Helping Your Kids

Anxiety 2 In 1

What Your Average Therapist Won't

Tell You About Your Kids Anxiety

By

D1073352

Lawrence Conley

Table of Contents

Anxiety Workbook For Kids

The Anxiety Cure For Kids

Little-Known Things That Might Worsen Your Kids Anxiety And How To Fix Them

By

Lawrence Conley

Introduction

Multiple statistical reports state that one in every four people would develop some anxiety disorder [1]. Children and teenagers are especially vulnerable to threats to their mental health. It happens because children are forced to live between two types of forces: biological and social.

In modern society, even young children can live under constant pressure. They feel that they are continually being evaluated by their family members, their teachers, and their friends. There are also expectations they learn about from the TV, the Internet, and other sources.

The rapid changes that the children's brains undergo during development also make them vulnerable. That is why the risk of mental disorders, especially anxiety, is so high in children [2].

Modern psychiatric research proves: pathological anxiety goes beyond the mere fear of bad grades or an attack from bullies [1, 2]. It can have a profound effect on the child's life, making it impossible for him or her to function and communicate normally [1 - 3]. The mounting evidence gathered in 20 years also proves that high levels of anxiety are also associated with the risk of developing depression at the same time or later in life [4].

It is proven without a doubt that anxiety is dangerous for the well-being of our children. Sometimes it seems that nothing can battle this constant dark cloud that hangs over your child. You want to protect them and help them, but do not know how.

Do we need to rely on specialists and counselors for help? Or are there methods that parents themselves can apply to help one's child to feel less fear, be happier, and be more resilient?

Here is at least part of the answer. And this answer is completely scientific. You can be assured it is based both on a lifetime of research and practical experience.

Drawing from multiple sources, we offer an algorithm of sorts to counteract this enemy of a happy childhood.

Of course, multiple treatment options can be suggested for mental disorders by medical professionals. There are genuinely effective therapies offered at medical facilities. There are also medicines aimed to help with overcoming anxiety. But this type of help is not enough.

You see, it is the parents that children view as their safe havens, their fortresses. We, as parents, provide the safety blanket against the scary things life presents. So, it falls to us to join hands with therapists to help children overcome their fears, both rational and irrational.

It is not hard to do. This book is going to prove it, step by step.

In the following chapters, we are going to offer you some crucial bricks in building a formidable defense structure against the anxiety threat. Even scientists acknowledge the importance of parental support in the prevention and treatment of anxiety disorders [5; 6]. The interventions at home can supplement the traditional lines of treatment and prevent possible risk of depression and suicide [6, 7].

Anxiety is our common enemy. To defeat it, you must understand it. To battle it, you can use several simple and effective strategies based on mindfulness, relaxation, and some critical thinking skills. All of these approaches are presented here.

This book is a comprehensive plan of action aimed to bring relief from anxiety for the young ones, backed up by science and practical experience. Considering the risk mental disorders pose, such as the development of severe depression, inability to function in society normally, and even the possibility of suicidal behavior, we must act now [5]. And this book is your weapon in this, sometimes uphill, battle.

Chapter 1. What Is Anxiety

Know Thy Enemy

In the course of our lives, we often feel anxiety. It is a normal response that helps us survive. Anxiety can be interpreted as an anticipation of a threat [8].

For example, we are aware of an event that may potentially cause us trouble occurring soon. It could be something as simple as an unpleasant meeting or an exam. As this event is troublesome and likely has unpleasant consequences (i.e., lousy grade at an exam), our body needs to prepare in advance. As a result, our heart rate increases, our muscles tense, the skin is covered with sweat.

We do not need sweaty palms at a meeting or exam! Unfortunately, our bodies may not understand the intricacies of social norms. It just knows that we are afraid of what is to come. And if we fear it – it counts as a threat.

Based on thousands of years of ingrained instincts, our body definitely knows what to do when a threat is expected. We must be either prepared to run away or to fight until the danger passes. That is why even if we do not meet real predators at a conference. The feelings associated with it may be very similar to the way a hare feels when it expects to meet a tiger [8].

The body switches gears inside that make us ready to run and also helps us to be as slippery as possible to evade capture – that is why we feel jittery and sweat a lot [9]. All of these processes happen to everyone – the difference is in how long they persevere inside us.

In the typical situation, when something unpleasant is no longer here – we instantly feel better. Our heart rate slows down, our muscles relax, and we may even feel elated. That is all part of the same mechanisms of self-defense we have inherited from our ancestors.

If we look at a mental disorder, the preparations our body makes for some instances refuse to fade away. The feelings usually reserved for threat anticipation persist and grow out of proportion. That is what happens in pathological anxiety – the fight or flight response would urge you from inside, even if there is no threat at all [8].

At times there is some threat, but the reaction is too severe for the risk before us. It is something like using an atomic bomb when a hand grenade would have been sufficient [8].

One of the reasons why children are especially likely to develop anxiety disorders is the fact that fears are a normal part of their lives [10]. Young children, both because of their age and dependence on adults, fear a lot of things, from ghosts to spiders [10].

Underlying fears of childhood are mostly a part of the child's self-protection [8]. But children's minds are not capable of critically evaluating the possible danger level. Many different things influence their views, from scary fairy tales to genuinely traumatic events.

Because children are not critical enough and lack knowledge about certain situations, their fears may grow out of proportion. Unstable environments and a lack of ways to change the situation make them feel increasingly helpless, frustrated, and scared. All these processes contribute to the development of anxiety disorders in young children [11-12].

All this is theory. In reality, as parents, we are observers and cannot regularly measure heart rates and other characteristics in our children. It would not do any good and would likely add another stressful experience. Then how are we supposed to tell if our child has chronic anxiety? Moreover, there is more than one kind of anxiety disorder – how can we tell them apart?

What Types Of Anxiety Disorders Are There?

Pathological anxiety comes in varied forms. According to the Diagnostic and Statistical Manual of Mental Disorders, Fourth Edition, there are several types of anxiety disorders with specific symptoms [3]. Some types of disorders are more likely to develop in childhood, while others are more typical for adolescents [1]. Let us look through several cases to understand the differences between them.

1. **Luke, aged 6.** Luke was always an introverted child. He had only two friends he preferred to play with, and he was very attached to his toys. One day, a bully on the playground took away his beloved teddy bear. He tore apart its arm and threw it into the mud. Luke was very shaken and cried a lot. To complicate matters, his parents were forced to transfer him to another preschool. With time, Luke became increasingly anxious and nervous. He was always worried about his toys. He also began to worry about his clothes. He was still afraid that someone would take his things, or someone would

hurt him. He began to have trouble sleeping. He used to go to a dancing class, but he became worse at dancing. His legs felt leaden; he could not stretch properly or do other exercises. He was forced to stop, and that has made him unhappy.

These are the approximate symptoms of **generalized anxiety disorder** [12]. The main symptom is a constant, persistent worry about a variety of things. The affected children also have problems with relaxing. They are always tense, take too long to fall asleep or have nightmares. The patients with this condition also feel constantly tired and irritable.

2. **Daisy, seven years old.** Daisy has always been a sensitive, caring girl. She loved her family a lot. She was used to sleeping with her mom. But when she has started school, her grandmother died. The teacher at school was also overly strict. Daisy became increasingly clingy. She began to follow her mother everywhere and refused to go out alone-

even to the nearest playground. She could not sleep by herself. Her parents even noticed that she began to invent stories that would prevent her mother from going out, too.

Daisy seems to be suffering from **separation anxiety** [11]. Younger children – toddlers, for instance - often depend on their parents and cling to them. But when a child gets over a certain age, this dependence should slowly subside. If one's child begins to feel an unexplained, irrational fear that something would happen to his/her loved ones, becomes nervous even if the parent goes to another room, or are scared to go out to play, it is time to consult a specialist.

3. **Lily, 11.** When Lily moved to a new school, her behavior suddenly changed. She became terrified of public speeches. It had gotten so bad that she would vomit or faint when she was forced to answer before the entire class. During her recesses, she tries to evade attention and rarely converses with friends.

Possibly, Lily has social anxiety disorder [12]. It often happens in teens. At this age, approval from peers and teachers becomes increasingly essential, and it often causes a fear of embarrassment, of doing something wrong.

People tend to avoid things that they fear – so teens suffering from social anxiety avoid gatherings and avoid attracting attention. It may become so severe that some children would be scared of talking on the phone or ordering food at a café.

4. **Josh, 10.** Josh has been living at a foster home because of an unpleasant family situation. After living at a new house for several months, he has started to have strange attacks. Suddenly, without warning, his head would start spinning, his heart would beat like mad, and he would have trouble breathing. A local pediatrician did not find anything

wrong with the boy's heart and lungs. No allergies or brain damage was diagnosed either.

Josh was having panic attacks [12]. Such attacks often happen out of the blue, without warning. They can be similar to heart attacks or asthma and can be so severe that the children may need urgent help. The condition when panic attacks happen regularly without any obvious trigger is called a panic disorder [12].

5. **Trixie, 8.** Trixie has always disliked high places. But in the last five months, she began to fear them. She could not even look out of the second-story window without her head spinning and feeling nauseous. She felt as if she would fall to her death any minute.

Trixie has developed a specific phobia [12]. Many people have fears or phobias. In normal circumstances, one avoids something that is feared.

But in some cases, the fears win and can become so out of control they even trigger panic attacks.

6. **Rose, 12.** Rose cannot stay in crowded places for long. She also prefers to avoid closed spaces. She cannot even stay in a classroom for a long time and needs to be homeschooled. When she is forced to remain in a closed or crowded room for a long time, she would breathe heavily and have heart palpitations. She often would complain afterward she was afraid she would die.

Rose has developed agoraphobia, the fear of closed spaces. People that have agoraphobia are likely to get panic attacks and faint when faced within a closed-up room. They also experience an intense fear of death in such situations, a feeling that there is no way out for them.

7. **James, 13.** James loves scientific experiments. But he is very particular about how to organize

them. All his instruments have to be in a specific order and sorted by size and color. His textbooks and notebooks are sorted in a similar fashion. James loves his laboratory. He has organized it himself in a separate wing of his house. He keeps it extremely clean. He prefers to stay there as much as possible. When James is having dinner with his family, he also tries to organize utensils and dishes. He dislikes leaving his lab for a long time. He begins drumming, fidgeting, touching his hair when he is kept from it too long.

James has a mild case of obsessive-compulsive disorder [12]. Patients with this condition rely heavily on their routine. Having everything in perfect order gives them a feeling of control. That is why they are obsessed with cleanliness, orderliness, may be afraid of germs, and have other similar symptoms.

As you can see, most anxiety disorders are based on

specific fears or worries that children usually have. But why do these fears grow so much that they cause physical pain?

To understand the transformations of rational fears, we need to look into the biological and psychological mechanisms in charge of our deep-seated reactions.

Chapter 2. Why Do We Worry?

What causes this destructive torrent of worry inside us? Human bodies, especially their brains, are very complex. Our reactions are determined by multiple mechanisms, including:

- Central nervous system activity;
- Chemical processes inside our bodies, ruled by hormones and neuromediators;
- Slight changes in our genes;
- Our perceptions of the world around us.

Let us look into each of the mechanisms closely.

We Worry Because Of Our Brains: Neurobiological Mechanisms Of Anxiety.

Mental health was not studied on a deep, neurobiological level until recently [13]. Recent research has helped us tremendously with understanding disorders based on fear (including anxiety and related conditions) [13]. Part of the reason those disorders develop is disruption of the standard mechanisms in the brain [13].

To better understand what is happening to our children, we would need to have a basic understanding of necessary neurobiological information: why those disruptions occur and where they are located. We would take a short detour and dive into some of the mysteries of the brain.

The brain has multiple regions, and usually, each one is assigned a specific function. Given our wish to understand the mechanisms that generate anxiety, we would need to zoom in on one in particular-the amygdala [14].

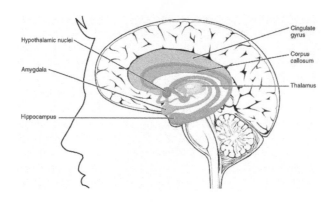

Pic. 1. This is the region called the limbic system – with the amygdala right above the hippocampus. Image: Wikimedia Commons.

As demonstrated in Pic. 1, the amygdala is located in the deep brain region. Together with several other structures, the amygdala forms the so-called limbic system [14]. It also serves as headquarters: receiving, interpreting, and sending our "orders." The primary function of the limbic system is generating emotions.

Part of the reason for the amygdala's power is the presence of multiple connections to significant brain areas. For instance, this area is connected to the hypothalamus, hippocampus, and neocortex [14]. All three structures are responsible for essential functions:

- **Hypothalamus** controls our hormones – those that regulate heartbeat and stress in particular;
- **Hippocampus** is vital for memory;
- **Neocortex** is the region that makes us human: it is where all complex associations occur [14].

Let us see how the amygdala switches on the fear response.

Our senses send new information to the amygdala regularly.

Amygdala interprets the newly arrived information as a threat.

Using all the above connections, it immediately sends

new orders to various structures.

Multiple "telegrams" are sent out simultaneously: the hypothalamus is told to increase the heart rate and blood pressure, while some brain areas are told to control attention or to trigger rapid breathing [14].

The amygdala continuously controls the threads of information, ready to send out new orders if the threat is gone.

The situation described above is what happens when everything is going as it should. In the case of anxiety disorders, though, this orderly process is disrupted. There are several possible versions:

- The reactions get out of control and persist even if the threat is past;
- The reactions are too severe compared to the danger presented;

– The fear reaction appears if there is no visible threat.

Why does it happen?

Scientific research cannot say for sure, but the specialists do have some hints [15]. To understand how the emotional state and brain activity are related, several brain imaging studies were carried out in people with several types of anxiety disorders [15-16].

Several experiments have helped us understand how mental disorders are linked with specific brain areas. Here are some examples:

Case Study 1. Panic disorder. Scientists followed the flow of glucose in the brains of panic disorder patients. Glucose is a crucial source of energy for the brain. When the brain cells in a particular area "gulp down" sugars – it means they are very active. In patients that had panic disorder, the amygdala, hippocampus, thalamus, and midbrain were taking up more glucose than the same areas in healthy people [16].

Case study 2. Social anxiety. People diagnosed with social anxiety were given photos with unpleasant faces. The images were used to elicit negative emotions in the participants.

As a result, it was found that the amygdala in social anxiety patients was taking up significantly more glucose than people without anxiety [15].

Case study 3. Diving deeper into social anxiety. In the course of this particular experiment, participants suffering from anxiety disorders were given unique scenarios that modeled situations that could cause anxiety. The brain imaging analysis has revealed some specific areas in the brain that get activated in response to feeling anxious [17]. These areas were located in the neocortex and were responsible for various complex functions [17].

Case study 4. Generalized anxiety disorder in children. Brain structure was compared between children with generalized anxiety disorder (GAD) and children with no mental health problems [18]. It was found that children with GAD had higher developed amygdala regions compared to children without the disorder. Their brains also contained more gray matter compared to others [18]. This finding may explain the exaggerated reactions these children may have to the events around them.

As these studies show, changes in the amygdala or its increased activity is the underlying cause of increased worry that leads to disorders. It was further proven in the course of another experiment.

Case study 5. Amygdala connections. According to another finding, the connections between the amygdala and certain regions of the neocortex were weaker in children with anxiety [18]. These same regions were also crucial in reactions to social situations [17]. The scientists propose that the lack of coordination and "dialogue" between regions may have led to a situation when the children could not recognize the difference between severe threats and insignificant ones [18].

Case study 6. The ruler of the amygdala. It was found the amygdala itself has a ruler called the ventromedial prefrontal cortex (VmPC) [15]. VmPC, together with some assisting regions regulates attention, orientation towards a threat and also evaluates the level of danger [15].

The influence of VmPC in anxiety was shown in a group of anxious children. These children were given the photographs of their classmates and had to decide with whom they would like to converse and with whom they wouldn't [19]. Then they had to wait for the evaluation from the children that they rated as unlikable previously [19].

While the children were awaiting results, they had undergone brain scanning [19]. The level of oxygen in different brain regions was also evaluated [19].

It was discovered that in this group of children, both the amygdala and the VmPC was activated [19]. Also, the connections between VmPC and amygdala were stronger in children with anxiety compared to the healthy control group [19].

VmPC also plays a crucial role in generalized anxiety disorder (GAD) [18]. According to brain imaging research, the severity of GAD is connected to the level of activation of this region [11].

In short, anxiety disorders are in part caused by abnormal activation of the brain regions responsible for reactions to fear, emotions, and regulating complex behaviors.

Many children with anxiety also have brains that develop at a different pace (it often happens during adolescence), which results in certain areas having more gray matter – i.e., nerve cells – and therefore becoming more active. Another consequence of such development is the appearance of unusually strong connections between certain regions, which can result in changes in behavior [20].

Besides the structure and links between the parts of the brain, chemical substances that the body also produces influence behavior [20]. For example, some hormones are directly controlled by the hypothalamus [20]. The hypothalamus, in its turn, is also involved in fear reactions [20]. Therefore, imbalance in those hormones may be one of the reasons for anxious behavior [20].

There is a vast array of steroid hormones, neurotransmitters, and other substances that during certain conditions could trigger anxiety [20]. For example, steroid hormones such as estrogens and testosterone can, in certain situations, either defuse anxiety or trigger in experiments on laboratory animals [20].

It is also thought that decreased activity of a neurotransmitter called GABA may also lead to certain types of anxiety disorders. For example, panic disorder and generalized anxiety disorders [15].

Other substances that influence the activity of nerve cells, such as serotonin, norepinephrine, and dopamine, were shown to suppress anxious feelings instead [15].

As we can see, the neurological basis of mental disorders is very complicated. Though it is good to keep in mind all the physiological, inner processes that happen, it is equally important for us to understand what external factors can trigger anxiety and how our feelings are involved in this process.

Predestination Vs. Environment

Many processes in the brain that we have described above are controlled genetically [21].

A nation-wide survey was carried out in Sweden, during which the scientists looked at the presence of anxiety disorder – related conditions in families. [21].

They have found that parents suffering from any anxiety disorder are highly likely to have children having similar mental health problems [21].

On the one hand, anxious parents can have anxious children because of a specific environment at home. On the other hand, many scientists consider there is a common trait that makes people more likely to develop eating disorders, depression, or different kinds of anxiety disorders [22]. The likelihood of developing anxiety was also linked to certain personality traits, such as neuroticism [21].

There are so-called Big Five personality traits that make each person unique [23]. They are Neuroticism, Extraversion, Openness, Agreeableness, and Conscientiousness [23]. And neuroticism may be the crucial trait that predisposes a person to anxiety [23].

Neuroticism is a typical trait of a "worrier." A neurotic person usually worries more or feels sad more often than an average person [24].

Personality can in part be inherited, and recently, a genome sequencing study done on 106,000 people have allowed scientists to find nine genes potentially carrying the neuroticism trait [22].

One of them, CRHR1, was also shown to be related to the likelihood of developing anxiety [22].

Not only personality traits related to anxiety are heritable; certain features of the brain can be passed down through generations, too. For example, rhesus monkeys that have inherited a brain with an amygdala overactive in certain regions were also more likely to have an anxious temperament [25].

But are genes everything? It is, of course, good to know that a child of a parent with a history of anxiety or depressive disorder may also develop something similar. But it does not mean all children that have such genes would. It is merely a risk factor.

As much as we are the product of our genes, we are also a product of our environment in the same measure.

And the main environmental factors contributing to

the development of anxiety are also the factors that elicit fear.

Some of the fears we feel are inborn. Others are learned [27-28]. Here are the main three ways to learn fear:

1. Classic, or Pavlov conditioning.

You may have read about Pavlov who studied reflexes in dogs. It works the same way in humans. For example, when we learn that touching a hot object leads to scalding and burns – it is a classic example of Pavlov conditioning.

This mechanism has one hidden loophole, though. It is called paired association [28]. This mechanism would be the reason for associating something harmless with something terrible.

Paired association can take place when,

accidentally, something that does not cause harm accompanies an unpleasant, threatening situation [28].

For example, if a person once had a severe panic attack at a bookstore, and the reason for the panic attack is not clear, the person would begin to avoid bookstores just in case.

Paired association is a frequent cause of anxiety in children. For instance, when Molly's Grandma died, her beloved teddy bear got lost. Now Molly is carrying her teddy bear everywhere and is mortally scared of losing him or damaging him because she associates the grief over the loss of her Grandma with the absence of the toy.

2. Vicarious fear learning [27].

A person does not need to experience something to know it is dangerous. It is sometimes enough to see that someone besides you deems something as a threat. Here are some experimental case studies to show this point.

Case study 1. Infants and toddlers.

Young children rely on their mothers to understand what to fear. An experiment that involved mother-child pairs was carried out to understand this process [29]. In the course of the research, the pairs were given images of animals. If the mother was showing a positive reaction – for example, smiling - the children also accepted the image. When the mother reacted to the image with fear – the child would avoid the picture [29].

Case study 2. Schoolchildren and guinea pigs [30].

In older children, fear learning also relies on the reactions of their peers, their play friends. In the course of another study, children were given pictures of two types of guinea pigs – one fluffy and one bald [30].

The children observed how other kids in the group reacted to the images. Then the children were led to a table with a toy farm and given two figurines. One figurine depicted a guinea pig similar to the one in the image (fluffy/bald) and a figurine of a child of the same gender as the participant. Then the children were asked to house both the animal and the "mini-child" on the farm.

It was discovered that children would place the "human" figure as far as possible from a guinea pig if they saw that the other children were scared of it. Basically, they have learned to fear the initially harmless creature just because others were showing fear of them [30].

3. **Passing down the negative information** [27].

We encounter this type of fear learning all the time: from reading scary stories to the children to reading news as adults. Many manipulations in the press are based on this mechanism.

In short, we worry because of several factors:

1. Our brain composition;
2. The genes we carry;
3. Our personalities: neurotic personality and low confidence are the most likely risk factors;
4. Fears that we have learned through our lives.

All those factors are intricately linked because there is a distinct relationship between our thoughts, our feelings, and changes in our bodies and behavior.

Chapter 3. The Link Between Thoughts, Feelings, And Anxiety

We know now several factors determine the presence of anxiety. Still, besides complex biological reasons for it, there is another crucial part of this puzzle – personal feelings and perceptions.

What does influence our feelings? As we look around, we see many things, and they elicit different feelings in us. Seeing a blooming tree makes us happier; seeing an overflowing rubbish bin makes us disgusted. And in an anxious person, seeing a crowd would make him or her scared and nervous.

But it is more complicated than that. Everything we see, we also think about daily. It is this "processing" with thoughts that would influence our reactions [31].

For example, the same blooming tree would get different reactions from different people depending on what they think about it. Compare:

- "Oh, what a beautiful tree! And it smells good, too! How wonderful!"
- "Well, is it that season already? Now I will have to buy my allergy medicine again!"

In the first case, the person would feel happy. In the second case, the person would be anxious and fearful because he or she is allergic to something in the blooms.

Our feelings are intimately connected to our thoughts. Moreover, our thoughts do not only control feelings. They also may control reactions in the body. How is that possible?

Our brains are made in a way that even a thought of the potential threat can trigger a typical "fight or flight" or "anxious" reactions.

Now, based on what we have already read, imagine that a person has one of those persistent fears. Such fears may have been inspired by something unpleasant in the past, or something learned to fear based on reactions or words of others. For example, propaganda on TV or the Internet).

Every time we see things that remind us of these fears or would make us expect something dangerous, we would feel the full blast of typical bodily reactions.

But here is the thing. It all depends on our interpretation.

We THINK those objects are dangerous. We do not know it for a fact or based on personal experience. But at the same time, we think those things MAKE us feel fear when, in reality, we control our feelings with our thoughts [31].

From this angle, our thoughts influence our bodies. And we have another problem – there are conscious thoughts, and there are automatic thoughts.

The latter is just like a never-ending commentary on the events around us and inside us. And if a person develops a persistent fear, it would be the first thing on this automatic tape, because worries are high on the priority lists inside our brains.

Let us follow the path of pathological worry inside our brains.

How Worry Moves In, How It Grows And Why Does It Need To Go

Usually, it is quite reasonable for the concern to come. As we plan and anticipate something, we also try out different ways things can go wrong. It actually can be a form of avoidance behavior – we identify something we fear and invent an approach on how to avoid it. For example, if we are worried, we would fail an exam we would spend more time preparing and read additional books to gain more knowledge. In this way, worrying helps us.

But sometimes, worrying does not go away. Especially when we worry about things we have no control over. For example, students may be concerned; the teacher may not like their homework, or their speech would not be accepted well by their classmates.

Sometimes these children have extremely low confidence in their abilities. In such cases, they, on the one hand, worry about the grade and acceptance they receive. On the other, they already believe they would fail. This way, the worry, and fear enter the loop of automatic thoughts, adding to the classic fear reaction drop by drop, just as we have described earlier.

What are the consequences of these worry loops? They are numerous.

First and foremost, the worry distracts us and makes us unable to focus. Can you work well when people play loud music nearby? In the same way, the brain cannot work and concentrate properly. There are even several reasons for this:

- **Constant thinking consumes energy**. The brain cells helping you think to drink up sugars, and the other regions of the brain may not get enough nutrients;
- **The body gets busy.** Through worry and anxiety, multiple processes in the body continuously get switched on. The brain cannot spend resources and power to support other regions responsible for your daily routines and work;

As a consequence of the above processes, your worry brings harm to your body. The bodily reactions triggered by worry are not only painful, but they also change the way your body works. That is why people that tend to worry a lot are more than likely to get such unpleasant conditions as gastritis or irritable bowel syndrome, fatigue, and nausea [32].

Conclusion: excessive worry and anxiousness damages our health and interferes with our regular life. Moreover, unlike short-term, functional worry, it does not help us reach our goals at all. Therefore, it needs to go away and be replaced with feelings and thoughts that make us happier and healthier.

Why Do Some People Worry More?

Have you noticed that some people live their lives as if they fly through each day? If something goes wrong, they have a strong belief it would somehow work out. And sometimes it does. There are also people whose outlook on life is quite the opposite.

We are talking about the group of people that are sometimes called "worrywarts." They obsess over everything, check and re-check every plan and prepare for every contingency. They are usually tense and anxious.

Many of these people are perfectionists tending to control everything and putting very high demands on themselves.

There are various reasons why people develop such a personality. First, there are genetic factors, though research shows that heredity does not contribute to anxiety development significantly [33]. Some of such elements are inborn personality traits, as we have seen earlier.

The other huge factor is the environment. When people live in constant stress, they would naturally worry more.

One important factor, especially in children, is the

behavior of their parents [34]. If the children feel insecure in their home environment, they would naturally view the whole world as unsafe, too. And it does not have to be abuse.

There is a type of parenting called "helicopter" parenting or, as scientists say "intrusive" parenting [34].

Parents of this type tend to control every aspect of the child's life. You can recognize such parent-child relationships if you see a parent and the child doing some task that is slightly harder for the child of this particular age [34].

Usually, parents tend to do such a task together with the child equally, or even wait until the child asks for help. An intrusive parent does not even give the child a chance to make a mistake, starting to do it all for him or her [34].

What would happen when the child has to grow in such an environment? Where he or she is controlled and has no right to vote over everything? It leads to an increasing feeling of frustration and helplessness. Anxiousness comes as a logical consequence. Anxiousness and helplessness are also triggered when parents are inconsistent with their emotions and the assignment of punishments.

Uncertainty, lack of confidence, and constant pressure are all things that would start a loop of worry in one's mind. This transforms a growing child into a worrier and contributes to the development of the anxiety disorder [35].

Certain kinds of environment can also force a child to suppress his or her emotions. It is critically destructive for his or her psychological state, especially when there is no outlet for the feelings.

What Happens When We Hide Our Fears And Worries?

Instead of a scientific case study, I'd like to tell you a regular story. My daughter was very open about everything when she was a toddler. When she was afraid of something – a bug, a fly, a wave – she cried, ran to someone she trusted, and stayed there until she could calm down.

As she grew older, the situation has changed. She would still run from the bees or flies, but there were some deeper fears that she was reluctant to express. Sometimes, she would hold my arm, almost trembling. Despite us asking her what is wrong, she never explained adequately. In all other aspects, she was a very open, communicative child.

With time, she began getting nightmares. They were awful. She would wake in the middle of the night, and she would cry non-stop. Sometimes she would talk of the things that were not there.

We were desperate. We went to her pediatrician, to a neurologist, and eventually to a counselor. She was even prescribed some potent drugs that were meant to calm her. We thought we would need to keep her on them. Until one day, when we were sitting together, she suddenly asked me: "You won't die, right?" The answer to her problems was simple: she has learned that people can die. And then she realized her parents are getting older, and they may die, too. But she was scared to voice it. She had this fear of her mom and dad leaving her, but she never expressed that fear.

But the fears had to go somewhere, and that is why she had begun to have sleeping troubles. She did not need strong drugs. She needed to feel safe enough to discuss her fears with the people she loved and trusted.

When thoughts are not let out, like birds from the cage, they tend to take away the joy and energy from you, in both a physiological and psychological sense. And they also make one's brain overactive. That is why my daughter's constant worrying led to bad dreams at night.

There can also be other consequences: changes in behavior, constant fatigue, inability to focus on anything besides those voices in your head. It can also lead to illness. The more secret feelings we suppress, the more we damage ourselves.

To break the loop, we need to confront our thoughts. And then step by step, change them and make them work FOR you, not AGAINST you. As we already know, fears appropriately used can be useful, after all.

Chapter 4. Educate Yourself And Your Child About Anxiety

First, one must realize that anxiety-related disorders are quite common. They can develop in everyone; there is mainly a significant risk of developing such disorders if there are some additional factors, such as:

- Death in the family;
- A move to another area;
- Start of the school (or school transfer);
- Frightening events in the area (for example, a fire, a crime, etc.);
- Constant pressure (for example, before the exams or in the highly competitive school);
- Conflicts in the family or with the nearest circle (teachers or friends);
- Recent physical trauma or a substantial illness.

All these factors are possible fuel for negative thoughts. Still, being in a tough situation does not automatically mean one would immediately develop anxiety. It merely means there is a potential risk.

If you are aware that your child is at risk for anxiety because of the described above instances, it would be a good preparation to read about the anxiety disorders beforehand. This way, you would know and loof for the symptoms.

If your child is at risk for anxiety, it is imperative to explain the condition to him/her as well. This way, you help your child in becoming more involved with his/her own life. They would also realize that there is nothing bad attached to an anxiety disorder. Having a mental illness is often a stigma, a "crazy" label. Proper education would help against that.

Why is it so crucial to understanding what anxiety is? Mainly because our mental health is just as important as our physical fitness. Our thoughts and feelings are precious because they make us who we are. And we humans are incredibly complex beings. Far more complicated than a regular computer.

We know that complex gadgets break more easily than simpler ones. That is why we try to understand how they work so we can repair them. In a way, such disorders as GAD or social anxiety is a type of break in our inner smartphones, a system overload in some of the apps. We need to recognize that the error occurred, why it happened, and then find the software that helps in setting everything right.

Chapter 5. Parenting With Empathy, Empathy For Confidence

Any person needs a safe environment. It is especially true for young children, as they rely on their families and do not have many tools to protect themselves. That is why parents need to provide a haven at home. When children know that there is a warm, accepting home waiting for them after any disaster, everything becomes much less scary and much more bearable.

Creating a safe home for your children does not only mean to protect them physically or provide for them financially. Parents or caregivers also have to care for the emotional needs of their young charges.

This task is significantly more complicated than just providing a growing person with food, shelter, and protection against threats. We would love to protect our beloved children from emotional pain the world throws their way, but our children still need to interact with their peers, their children, and others outside the family circle. We cannot isolate them to prevent their suffering. Instead, we must teach them how to interact with society, how to obey its rules, and how to bounce back after unpleasant accidents. Children need to develop resilience – an ability to rebuild after a shock. As this is not a new problem in raising children, several parenting styles supposedly would help with resilience development.

Recent research has shown that not all parenting styles are equally successful [35]. The specialists determine several parenting styles [35]:

- Authoritative – parents are both warm and demanding;
- Indulgent – parents are warm and not demanding;
- Authoritarian (demanding without being warm);
- Negligent (neither demanding nor warm).

Recent research has revealed that the best parenting style to prevent behavioral problems is the indulgent parenting style [36]. Though the initial description seems counterproductive – people would suppose that indulgence would lead to spoiling the child – its efficacy is proven regularly by research throughout Europe [36].

Why is the indulgent style successful? Because this approach is built on empathy. Here are the main components of genuinely empathetic parenting [38]:

1. **An empathic parent listens to the child.**

   We all need a sympathetic ear, and even the smallest children are no exception. The child must know that whatever happens, he/she can talk to you about it. It also shows the child that their thoughts and feelings matter, and it helps build self-esteem.

2. **An empathic parent always takes the child's feelings seriously.**

   Children tend to overreact. It is normal. For many

children, even a small bruise or a broken doll is not far from the end of the universe. When you dismiss their disappointment, sadness, and fear – they feel as if you reject them entirely. So it is crucial to acknowledge their feelings and their right to feel upset. Only after you show them that you care, you can proceed to explain that this particular problem can have a simple solution.

3. An empathic parent is ready to take responsibility together with the child.

We are not always perfect. We can often be tired and upset and take it out on our nearest circle. But you need to acknowledge your own mistakes, too. This way, you show your child that they can expect justice and respect from you.

4. An empathic parent allows the child to make mistakes.

You can't transplant your thoughts and experience into your kid's head. Of course, we would like our kids to be happy, and we would dearly love to protect them, to do everything for him/her. But it does not do any good in the long run. It just shows the child three things:

- You do not trust him/her;
- You think him/her incapable;
- You prevent anything good or interesting from happening;

When a child is confronted by a complicated situation or test, instead of doing everything instead of them, or taking them away from the situation, instead:

1. Ask if you can help;
2. Ask if he/she wants to try to do it independently;
3. If you think that doing something is dangerous, explain why clearly;

4. Explain the rules that would help protect the child (for instance – want to go to a building site? All right, but you should wear a helmet!).

Prohibiting something completely would work only if the child would be in considerable and irreversible danger that cannot be prevented by safety measures.

In other cases, try to mitigate the potential danger as much as possible (for instance, offer to wear waterproof clothes if the child wants to walk in the rain).

Respectfully negotiate, acknowledging the wishes and feelings of the opposite party.

Some rules should be applied in the case your child has already made a mistake:

1. Offer praise for things the child has achieved;

2. Remind your child that you accept them fully and unconditionally. Remember – your actions towards your children have to support your words!;

3. Discuss with your child why the mistake was made and his/her thoughts on the subject;

4. Irrespective of the number of errors made, encourage the child at what he/she wants to do and is interested in even if it is hard at first;

5. **Punishments must be consistent and without cruelty.**

The children may make mistakes in judgment and break specific rules.

But the punishments for breaking those rules must be consistent and reasonable.

A punishment's aim is for the child to correct the mistake, not to make the child feel bad and more guilty than necessary.

6. Always provide a safe place, no matter what.

The child must know that he/she would expect love, support, and acceptance at their parent's home. That even in case of big mistakes, these things would still be there. Consistent and warm treatment is a key component to both prevent anxiety and help remedy it if it has already developed [38].

Chapter 6. What Are Common Fears And Worries?

We experience fear at all stages of life. Let us look closely at what fear is.

While anxiety is the process of anticipation of a threat, fear is the direct reaction to the threat. Fear sends a signal to us – something is dangerous for our health and well-being. According to scientific thought [41], fear has three components: physiological symptoms, feeling of apprehension, and avoidance. Very similar to the elements to anxiety, is it not? There are several groups of fears:

1. Fear of animals (fear of spiders or bees is very common);
2. Fear of situations (for example, public speaking);
3. Fear of environment (closed spaces);
4. Fear of blood, injury, etc.

Fears for children are entirely normal. They start from infancy – babies are scared of loud noises, darkness, and separation from parents. As you can see, such fears are usually related to the child's environment. As the child grows, he/she also begins to get new fears. Each stage has its own. The fears at each stage reflect the process of understanding and making sense of the world around the child.

For example, a preschooler may be afraid of ghosts or the Sandman. If you think about it, preschoolers begin to discover the nature and all the new things around them. To gain some sense about the environment, the children rely on the stories we tell them – such as fairy tales.

Supernatural fears they feel as a result are typical for this age and are the side effect of this wonder at the world around them.

As the children start school and interact with the world

more, they begin to get other fears – of spiders, for instance. They begin to realize that some things pose the real danger for them: may bite, sting, cause a rash, or would lead to a nasty fall. Their fears reflect this adaptation to their surroundings.

When the child reaches his/her teens, the social relationships are becoming the most important – and so their fears are mostly situational: fear of exclusion, fear of the public, and other typical problems of these turbulent years.

Common fears experienced during development have one common feature: they are temporary. More often than not, your child would probably completely forget about a scary boogeyman living under their bed when elementary school starts. But if the fear remains, becomes exaggerated or a child begins to fear something potentially non–threatening – there is a cause for concern.

Chapter 7. Learning About My Fears And Worries

Sometimes our fears are not obvious. They are hiding under other things. For instance, a child begins to refuse to do homework, going to school, or going out at all. One may assume that the reason behind this is just laziness or probably game addiction. In fact, the child avoids anything school-related because he/she is afraid of failure, of being mocked by teachers or classmates. By avoiding any interaction with others, the child avoids the potential danger of ridicule.

It is essential to identify precisely the source of the problem. Here are some questions you could find the answers to yourself or do a questionnaire together with your child.

Study Your Fear Questionnaire

1. What do you hate doing?
2. What makes you nervous?

3. What do you know you are afraid of?

4. Is there something you want to do, but are scared to do so?

5. What do you dislike talking about?

6. How do teachers/doctors/policemen make you feel?

7. Do you think a lot about what others think about you?

8. Do you prefer things to be predictable?

9. Are you okay with surprises – when you do not know what to expect?

10. How do you feel about change?

11. Do you like being alone?

12. How do you feel about taking risks?

When doing this type of questionnaire, it is essential to discuss what the child feels and why he/she feels that way. For example, some apparent fears, like fear of the dark, may hide another, more deep-seated fear – fear of getting hurt, of death, of losing family. It is important to discuss and play around with each question.

It is also important to tread even more carefully with preschoolers. Instead of a complicated checklist, you can invent short stories or fairy tales to help the child identify the fears. Here is an example:

Zoey And The Bees.

There was a ladybug called Zoey. She was an adorable and pretty ladybug, but she was really, really afraid of bees. Whenever she saw a bee, she would quickly run under the leaf, or fly into a hollow tree, and hide there, trembling. But once she met an ant. This ant told her that bees are not at all interested in ladybugs. Bees only like nectar and pollen from flowers. They never attack anybody, unless someone attacks them or tries to steal their honey.

So the ladybug stopped being afraid of bees. She understood that their loud noises and strange color made her think they would attack her and sting her.

Moreover, the ladybug even made friends with some bees from the beehive nearby. She began eating pests that attacked the flowers her neighbor bees liked, so the flowers grew better, and the bees got more honey.

When a story is finished, it would be a good idea to make a small discussion.

Exercises After The Story:

After the tale, discuss with the child what they think of the ladybug, and whether they have similar fears. You can invent any stories that fit the questions above. The rules of catching the fear are:

1. The "real" fear is something the child would actively avoid;
2. The real fear is something that may prevent the child from doing what he/she likes;
3. The fear makes the child feel uncertain, nervous, anxious – even sick in some extreme cases.

If you find a topic that makes your child feel like that, then you may be on the right track. The important thing is not to pressure them and to stop the discussion when the child gets distressed and scared.

Chapter 8. Determine If Your Child Has An Anxiety Problem

To diagnose any mental disorder, specialists use specific manuals, such as a diagnostic and Statistical Manual of Mental Disorders [3]. They also employ multiple assessment methods [3]. But a specialist would not see a child randomly.

It is not always easy to realize that one's child requires professional psychological help. Significant adults in the child's life, such as parents, teachers, or a guardian must notice first that something is indeed wrong. So what signs of anxiety one can heed?

The rule of thumb in these cases is to remember that anxiety becomes pathological when it interferes with normal life. For example, it is normal for a child to fear spiders; but it is not healthy when a child refuses to venture outside because there can be a spider hidden somewhere.

Let us list the most common signs that point to a possible disorder:

Excessive physical symptoms of anxiety.

We have already mentioned that a normal anxiety reaction involves sweating, rapid heartbeats, and muscle tension. But these symptoms can escalate, and a child can become so nervous that:

- he/she complains of stomachache, nausea or even constipation;
- the child suffers from severe headaches, dizziness and sometimes even fainting;
- the child sometimes feels unable to breathe (when there is no underlying physical condition, such as a heart disorder or asthma).

1. **Psychological symptoms:**
    a. The child begins to suffer from nightmares regularly or is not able to fall asleep;

b. The child becomes overly "clingy" and continually needs the presence of a significant adult;

c. The child becomes overly shy and uncommunicative, or, in reverse, overly vocal or even aggressive.

2. **Other signs that show that the child's mental condition interferes with their life:**

a. The child stops showing interest in things he/she previously liked;

b. The child stops wanting to go to school or outside to play with friends;

c. The child loses their appetite.

As you can see, even unexplained stomach problems can become the first warning sign of a disorder. It is also essential to understand whether the behavior of your child is more negative or positive overall.

I want to explain it based on one particular behavior –

shyness [39-40]. Lately, psychology specialists have begun to differentiate between "positive" and "negative" shyness [39]. This type of behavior can even be observed in very young children or toddlers [39].

For example, some children, when getting to meet a new person for the first time, avert their eyes, turn their heads or use any other gesture to show they want to evade the person in question – but still smile and remain calm [39]. This is a "positive" shy behavior. But some children behave differently.

You have probably encountered toddlers that frown and even cry when meeting a new person. This type of shyness is considered "negative." Moreover, when your child exhibits "negative" shyness more often than the positive version, he/she is at higher risk of developing social anxiety later, according to research [40].

So while observing shyness, especially in younger

children, it is good to see how much the child tries to withdraw, and with what attitude. It can help catch early signs of an anxiety disorder.

The general approach in all cases is to put all behavior in perspective: how often does your child behave that way? Have they been displaying new habits for a long time? How drastic is the change compared to the past? It is also important to eliminate other possible valid reasons for the behavior changes, such as medical problems or psychological trauma (for example, the death of someone significant).

Of course, the last word belongs to a certified professional. A therapist or a mental advisor with a vast array of methods to ensure the child indeed has a mental disorder.

Want to have something more hands-on? Try to use the checklist based on suggestions from Anxiety.org website [41]:

Checklist

1. Does your child appear more restless than usual?
2. Has your child been getting frequent headaches, stomachaches, nausea?
3. Does your child appear more nervous and agitated than usual?
4. Does your child have problems with focusing on homework or other tasks?
5. Has your child started having meltdowns about going to school, clothes, homework?
6. Does your child have tantrums more often than usual?
7. Has he/she started finding excuses to not go to school/kindergarten/other activities?
8. Has your child been crying more than usual?
9. Does your child have trouble going to sleep or sleeping through the night?
10. Does your child set extremely high expectations for his/her schoolwork or sports activities?

11. Are your family members going through a transition – move to another home or divorce?
12. Were there any kinds of scary incidents recently?

Now, you should count how many times you have answered "yes." If there are more than five affirmative answers, there is a reason to be on alert. Something is indeed wrong.

The likelihood of your child being in the risk group of anxiety is higher if [42]:

- you know that he/she is prone to worry too much;
- if he/she is very ambitious, with extremely high goals for grades and sports;
- if your child always puts others before himself/herself;
- if your child is usually shy or having trouble communicating with new people.

If you have noticed some changes in health and behavior and also know that your child can be placed in one of the risk groups above it is time to sit down and begin working with your child through the things that may disturb them.

Thankfully, there is a whole toolbox of useful and simple exercises to use against the dragon of anxiety.

Chapter 9. A Toolbox Of Strategies

A carpenter has tools for repairing tables and benches. We would now walk through several mental exercises and meditations that would serve as a toolbox that could keep anxiety and worry at bay.

Mindfulness

Mindfulness is a complicated notion. It is a practice, a way of life that consists of several techniques based on teachings from Asia, mainly Buddhism [43]. The main idea that lies in the basis of the mindfulness approach is "being in the moment" [43]. This means being aware of your body, feelings, and sensations [43].

Mindfulness is different from approaches stemming from Western philosophy. The latter is focused on changing your thoughts. Mindfulness is not about change; it is about understanding your inner condition, accepting it, and letting go of anything you identify as harmful [43].

According to specialists, this approach has at least one significant advantage. When you suffer from an extreme fear of something, you do your best to avoid that fear. And those so-called avoidance strategies can be very disruptive. For example, fear of rejection or failure can lead to complete isolation from any social activity and relationships. By accepting your fear and letting it go, you: a) stop avoiding it; b) get a kind of exposure therapy, slowly getting used to the idea and thus lessening the fear itself, as a tolerance treatment one gets for allergies.

There are many kinds of treatment strategies nowadays based on mindfulness, and they fall under the umbrella term of mindfulness-based therapies, or MBT. According to research, using MBT for the treatment of mood and anxiety disorders has been consistently proven to be successful [44].

Practicing mindfulness requires specific preparations.

We cannot look properly inside our minds if we are influenced by the outside world and are not relaxed. So learning relaxation techniques is a first step for learning mindfulness. Relaxation is a necessity for treating anxiety, as well. An anxious person is a person that feels constant tension – so it is vital to eliminate this tension.

My Relaxation Ideas

Being relaxed is opposite to being worried; that is why learning to relax is crucial for our battle against anxiety.

And children need to be taught relaxation techniques from an early age. Think of what relaxes you or your child. Having a bath? Playing with toys? Walking in a green area? Does your child have an active imagination that could be used for some make-believe meditation?

Here are some ideas:

1. Playing with rocks. Rocks can be either plain or colorful. You can also use something like Orbeez;
2. Having a bath with bubbles;
3. Counting with closed eyes;
4. Lying down and imagining something beautiful: a safe castle, a meadow, anything your child would like;
5. Blowing bubbles;
6. Using toys or pillows with herbs inside, such as lavender and mint;
7. Playing with soft toys pleasant to the touch;
8. Building a fortress with toy bricks;
9. Talking a walk, trying to count as many different bugs/trees/flowers as possible;
10. Playing scented play-dough;
11. Using stress balls;
12. Listen to pleasant sounds (waves, beats, rainforest, etc.);
13. There is also a good technique called inversion [43].

To perform inversion, you need to place your head below your heart level. Handstands or bending over from a couch could do the trick. Stay in the inverted position for several seconds.

You do not have to use those particular relaxation techniques; by observing your child, you can choose something suitable for him/her individually. You can also read on and take your pick through some meditation ideas.

Body Scan

The body scan is a common relaxation technique often used during meditations. It helps release tension, stress, and anxiety. Here are the main steps [45]:

1. Lie down on something comfortable (a bed or a mat). You can do it sitting as well;
2. Close your eyes;
3. Begin taking deep breaths. Imagine that the air needs to come up from your belly, not your chest;
4. Start a mental checkup of your whole body. Your head is first to go;

5. Hold your attention at each part of the body, even a small one: ears, fingers, toes, etc.;

6. Check if you feel tension in any part of your body. Usually, it feels as if the muscles in the area are particularly tight;

7. When you catch a part with tension, focus on it. Imagine that tension slowly seeps away, leaving your muscle relaxed;

8. Do not forget to breathe evenly and regularly!;

9. After paying attention to all the problem areas, scan your body again;

10. You can finish when you can't manage to find any tension anywhere;

11. Slowly count to ten and open your eyes;

12. The stress and tension have flown away!

The key component for this meditation and a similar technique is proper breathing.

Deep Belly Breathing

Belly breathing is also called diaphragmatic breathing

[45]. How is it different from the way you usually breathe?

Close your eyes and put your hand on your chest. Observe how you breathe. When you breathe lightly, only your chest rises. Now observe yourself when you start deeper breaths. Do you notice how your belly also begins to rise and fall together with your chest? This is what you need to achieve.

In belly breathing, you involve several structures in breathing besides your lungs, including muscles of the stomach.

How to achieve this?

Step-By-Step Guide For Belly Breathing

1. Lie or sit comfortably;
2. Put one hand on your chest, while keeping the other on your belly;

3. Start breathing. Try to engage the muscles of your belly as much as possible;

4. If you are doing belly breathing correctly, the hand that is placed on your chest will remain steady, while the hand that you have placed on your belly would rise and fall.

What is the secret to belly breathing? As the name suggests, this type of breathing involves using the diaphragm, a special muscle that is located between the lungs and the digestive cavity. When we breathe, the diaphragm rises up and down, helping the lungs expand and take up oxygen and then release the air. When you breathe deeply, using your belly, you engage your diaphragm more, thus helping the lungs getting as much oxygen as possible. This oxygen then is used by all your organs, including your brain. By receiving more oxygen, your cells would also be able to get more energy. Moreover, calm, deep breathing helps you center yourself and become less nervous.

Muscle Relaxation

Constant anxiety means constant readiness for battle. And this also means constant muscle tension, as if the body is always ready to run or attack the imaginary threat. Some people exist in this tense state their entire lives, unable to even understand what relaxation means. They have never experienced feeling relaxed.

That is why it is essential to teach your child relaxation techniques. This way, the child would know his/her body much better and would be able to control their muscles. It would be an excellent tool for managing anxiety, as well.

One of the relaxation exercises you could practice together with your child is progressive muscle relaxation, as recommended by Anxiety Canada [45].

This technique consists of two significant steps. The first step is to start tensing your muscles group by group (hand, foot, arm, leg, stomach, etc.). The second step is to learn the opposite of tension and start relaxing each group of muscles in its turn. This technique teaches the difference between tensed and relaxed muscles. Mastering this cycle of tension and relaxation would take time. Still, if one does learn the technique, the benefits are achieved. You would be gaining actual control over your body instead of following its reactions.

Let us go through the main steps of this process.

1. Prepare for the exercise. For this you would need:
   a. Find a comfortable place to sit or lie down comfortably;
   b. Wear comfortable, soft clothes;
   c. Take your shoes off.

An important note: remember that this exercise in its slowest mode may take around 15 minutes. Organize your schedule in such a way there won't be any distractions. It would be good to put your phone in silent mode as well – no distractions or work calls!

2. Lie/sit down and close your eyes.

3. Begin to tense the chosen group of muscles. Start with your right foot, for example. Inhale. Tense the foot so that you would feel the tension. Hold it like that for about 15 seconds. Release the tension. Exhale. Continue:
   a. Right ankle;
   b. Right leg;
   c. Repeat on the left leg;
   d. Move to your hands and arms;
   e. Tense your stomach;
   f. Tense your chest (inhale to the maximum);
   g. Tense your neck and shoulders (put your shoulders up to your ears);
   h. Open your mouth as wide as possible;
   i. Put your eyebrows as high as possible (or put your face into a severe frown).

4. After you have tensed and relaxed your body from feet to head, it is time for the second part. Try to relax the target groups of muscles in the same order. For this, slowly exhale and imagine that the tension seeps outside. Hold this relaxed state for a few seconds, so that you would remember the right feeling.

5. After several weeks of practice, you may graduate to exercising bigger groups of muscles in this way: the entire leg/both legs, entire arm/both arms, stomach, chest, neck, and head.

6. When you have learned how relaxed muscles feel, one may skip the tension step altogether and focus on relaxing parts of your body or your body as a whole.

This exercise helps you become more in tune with yourself. Here are some additional safety tips:

- Never tense your muscles so hard that you would feel pain. This technique aims to feel better, not hurt!;

- This exercise can take a full 15 minutes. Some people may think that is too much time for their busy lifestyle. Still, this is a particular time you devote to yourself. So, it is good to add 5-10 minutes to allow yourself to transition from this new, relaxed state to your regular activity;

- It is better to perform this exercise sitting if lying in bed relaxed is putting you to sleep;

- You can use a special relaxation CD to help you with your routine. These CDs are either walkthroughs that help you do the exercise step by step; the others contain pleasant music – rainforest sounds, sounds of the sea or some classics.

Now, all that remains is to learn the technique yourself and then make a personal CD for your child. You can use a story to make the exercise more fun and inviting.

Stress Balls

There are several groups of symptoms that are typical of anxiety disorders [46].

One of the groups of symptoms is repetitive behaviors [47]. There are different kinds. Some children, for instance, constantly interact with their bodies – pick their nose or bite their nails. This type of behavior is called body-focused repetitive behaviors [47].

Other people interact with objects when they are feeling anxious – they click pens, tear paper, or even gnaw something. These repetitive behaviors are a way to reduce stress [48].

Such behaviors are as common in animals as in humans. Have you seen a lion constantly pacing his territory when he smells something strange? It is on alert but does not know what to expect, so it continually paces to feel some control [48].

Our repetitive behaviors serve the same purpose – to feel in control and to have an outlet for the energy generated in anticipation of a potential threat.

The problem is many of those behaviors are destructive. Children or adults with anxiety tend to destroy objects around them or their bodies. In other cases, they are so distracted by the necessity to repeat certain rituals that they cannot focus on other tasks.

The trick to overcoming those behaviors is to refocus them in a way that is more or less productive or at least less destructive. The simplest way to do so is to use stress balls.

A stress ball is usually a round, soft ball that is soft and pleasant to the touch. It can easily change shape. There is an outer, stretchable "shell" made from plastic and a soft "filling" composed of small beads or powder-like substances. Some stress balls are pleasant to touch and squeeze; others are made from sturdier materials – durable rubber, for instance. These items can also help build hand strength.

The first stress balls were invented in the 1980's. They were used for safer "rage release" – you could throw them, and they would bounce back without breaking or damaging anything.

Modern stress balls are less bouncy and tend to be stretchier. The main idea behind their use is to squeeze them repetitively to calm themselves.

Stress balls are not just fancy new items. They are used for serious purposes as well.

For example, there were reports that stress balls successfully served as distractions and helped reduce anxiety before conscious surgery [49-50].

In another study, it was established that stress balls help middle-grade schoolers be more attentive in class [51].

In short, stress balls do help. And what is even better – one can make them oneself!

There are multiple instructions on the Internet on producing your DIY stress balls [52]. Usually, you would need:

- A plastic balloon;
- Flour, cornstarch, orbeez balls;
- A funnel;
- A piece of string;
- A marker/felt pen.

You can play with these ingredients to produce a ball your child would like. It would be even better to create several, with different colors and contents.

There is another fashionable addition to the tools against anxiety and stress - fidget spinners. They do not improve hand strength, but they help improve the attention span and focus on students [53].

It does not matter whether your ball is manufactured or homemade. What matters is that such a simple trinket would help your child relax, be in control, and teach him or her to deal with mounting stress, uncontrolled rage, or anxiety.

Creating My Own Peaceful Place

While parents can become a haven for their children, they are not over powerful and have their limits. Also, there are times when a child needs to be alone. And there should be a nice, safe place for him/her to stay without distractions and disturbances. In ideal circumstances, it should be a separate, special area where the child would have an opportunity to become removed from the everyday stress and school responsibilities.

It is best to plan such an area together with your child. Here are some things you can discuss during planning:

1. **What would your dream place look like?**

   It can be anything: a tepee, a tent, a nook made of books. The form and the main idea should be dependent on your child's interests;

2. **Should this place be inside or outside?**

   Look around your house or apartment. A "safe place" should be installed in an area that can be easily avoidable by adults, to give the inhabitant some much-needed space. If you have a big enough yard or a garden, you can make a small gazebo in the backyard, place a tent, make a nook in the garage, or even build a treehouse. If space is limited, it is enough to organize a tent or a nook formed by colorful blankets, for example.

3. **What do you want to put inside?**

The contents are as important as the outer look for such a space. This space should be a feast for all the senses.

First, consider touch. The textures inside the space should be soft. Soft woolen blankets or a carpet, for instance (if the child is not allergic, of course).

Next is color. Of course, the colors should be based on the child's preferences, but they also should be muted and overly bright or neon.

The third notable instance is what your child considers precious. Favorite toys or small knick-knacks are essential for creating a comfortable atmosphere that makes the child feel loved.

Pictures of the people the child likes should adorn the walls, as well as something your child has made for their personal use.

4. What does your child like to do?

If he/she has hobbies like drawing, beading, or other handmade activities, the tools for them should have their prominent place as well.

In short, this should be a place where your child can be at peace and can do things that calm him/her down.

There are some important rules for such a place, though:

- There should be no technology inside, except maybe a source of sound;
- No loud music is allowed in such a place – only calming sounds, meditative music or classical music are permitted;
- The lighting should not be overly bright and safe. Therefore, candles or neon lights are not an option. Salt lamps and lamps with soft, muted light are preferred;
- It is good to install some sound protective equipment so that the child can be isolated from the outside noise and relax in silence;

– The only way an adult gets into the safe space is with the child's permission. The only exception is a serious emergency. It should be a completely safe space, where the child is allowed to be in control. Pets can be an exception – again if the child wishes it so.

Besides the items described above, a peaceful place can include:

– stress balls, feeling jars, other objects with pleasant textures;
– art books;
– plasticine or playdough (the kind that is safe and not particularly sticky);
– a couple of favorite picture books or one book that is most beloved;
– a bell or a small signal lamp that would make a sound/light up when someone enters. It could indicate the start and finish of the "unwind time" if the child has schoolwork or other responsibilities.

Do you like the description of a safe place and want to make one yourself? Why not? Having something like that is equally important for adults, too!

Mindfulness Meditation

Different meditation techniques are a great way to control one's anxiety. The efficacy of meditation-based therapies in anxiety relief was supported both by academic research and multiple clinical trials [54].

Adults learn proper meditation techniques for years and close themselves up in monasteries. If it is such a complex concept, can we teach meditation to children?

In this, we need to follow the experience of an average teacher. You cannot teach a new concept to anyone if you do not understand it yourself. We need to learn for ourselves the approach used in mindfulness teachings and the reasons for their effectiveness.

First, let us look into why mindfulness meditation is so effective. Unlike regular meditations, which involve relaxing and emptying oneself from any thoughts whatsoever, mindfulness meditation follows a different concept.

This type of meditation is a continuation of the whole mindfulness philosophy. Being mindful means being fully present in the current situation. As anxiety often involves worrying about past or future events, mindfulness is an ideal tool for counteraction. By centering the body and mind in the present, a person would be able to get a measure of control over those feelings and thoughts.

We must admit that we do not control the whirl of thoughts in our heads.

For example, have you ever had "thoughts about thoughts" that are triggered by specific events?

Or have you considered how much your opinions are influenced by outside forces, such as our upbringing or society's expectations? We may have formed independent opinions, but they are still the result of multiple experiences.

When you practice mindfulness meditation, you can distance yourself from those influences.

Another important part of the mindfulness worldview is also to be acceptive of what you are and what you feel and think.

Mindfulness is more than relaxation and calming down. Your anxiety is also reduced because you learn to stop judging and criticizing yourself.

Curiously, there are scientific studies that prove that mindfulness techniques go deeper than a mere psychological approach. They can also change the way our brains work [54-56].

In the course of the study carried out by Zeidan et al. [55], participants with anxiety had undergone MRT scanning before and after practicing meditation.

MRT scans have shown that in those who practiced meditation, certain brain areas were activated [55].

Those brain areas were responsible for emotion control and evaluation of information that is translated to the brain from our senses [55].

The participants also reported that they felt less anxious after practicing meditation [55].

In simple words, meditation helps in switching our brain into a more controlled mode, which can help significantly in anxiety disorder, when our feelings control us. Let us see how this can be done, step by step.

Mindfulness Meditation Steps:

1. Find a comfortable, peaceful place (maybe that beautiful, safe place we were discussing earlier).
2. Sit or lie down – whatever is comfortable.
3. Concentrate on your breathing. As we have mentioned earlier, it is handy to breathe from one's belly. To control if you are breathing correctly, put one of your hands on your belly. It should rise and fall with your breaths.
4. Observe how you breathe for a while.
5. Start registering your thoughts and feelings. Are you anxious? Angry? Bored? Imagine you are looking at each thought and feeling "in the face," so to speak. Then let it go.
6. You do not have to banish your thoughts. Instead, acknowledge whatever you are feeling and thinking without judgment.
7. If you feel you are getting distracted, catch your distraction "by the tail." What are you distracted

by? What are your thoughts and feelings on the subject?

8. Always remain calm and focus on your breathing. It helps you stay grounded.

9. Set a timer about 2 -3 minutes earlier than you intend to finish your meditation. Slowly "come to." Sit calmly for a while, as if you are entering reality again.

10. Slowly get up.

You can go through the steps together with your child. Make a story to use during the meditation. For example, suggest that the thoughts and feelings are of a fish. Let your child catch his/her fish, imagine their coloring, etc. It is also good to make a tape of the meditation steps and let your child play it when he/she wants, to practice meditation at his/her chosen peaceful place.

Remember that meditations are not limited by sitting. Look into meditations one can do while working or doing chores.

Bubble Meditation

Meditation does not have to be serious. One of the most child-friendly meditations is a bubble meditation. All you need for this exercise is a bottle of soap solution, a stick for blowing bubbles and an area where bubbles would not spoil anything (avoid expensive furniture or furnishings). And some free time!

1. Sit down with your bubble bottle.
2. Take a deep, belly breath.
3. When you exhale blow as many bubbles as possible. Or you can blow very slowly, trying to make one big, rainbow bubble.
4. Release the bubble and observe it for some time.
5. Repeat.

Blowing bubbles is not as simple as it looks. You need concentration. Otherwise, the bubbles could break.

Blowing bubbles is an excellent method of feeling grounded and in the present moment.

Small tip: experiment with different brands of bubbles. Some produce short versions, while others are great for blowing sturdy, long-lived bubbles one can observe for some time. There are also sticky bubbles for touch and play!

Brain Breathing

Oxygen is crucial for the normal functioning of the brain. Brain cells cannot generate energy without oxygen. In one experiment, it was shown that supplying people with additional oxygen with the help of an oxygen generator has significantly improved their memory [56]. To provide your brain with oxygen, you do not need to get a personal oxygen generator: you need to do breathing exercises regularly.

Here are some examples [57]:

1. **Breathing through the nose:**
   a. Sit down.
   b. Slowly breathe in through the nose.
   c. Wait until your lungs feel "full."
   d. Hold your breath for a second.
   e. Slowly exhale.

Tip: Try to count in your head until the "fullness" point. When you know for sure that, for instance, your "full" point is at the five mark, count to five for each inhale and exhale. It helps with calming down and centering oneself.

2. **Alternate nostril breathing:**
   This technique was borrowed from yoga.
   a. Sit down or stand up – be comfortable;
   b. Close one nostril and inhale deeply with the other;
   c. Close the "input" nostril and exhale through the other that was closed previously;
   d. Repeat.

Remember to do this exercise slowly. It is also good to count to pace the practices. You should do them neither too quickly nor too slow. This exercise is supposed to help you feel balanced, calm, and energized.

Breathing techniques would help your children in the future, too. Having simple exercises that would help them relax and have a short "brain boost" would be invaluable in many situations.

Making A Feeling Jar

Young children have significant difficulties in understanding their emotions and feelings. It is one of the reasons they are so vulnerable to anxiety. There is a helpful technique that assists them in untangling their feelings and thoughts about various situations.

What is the most challenging thing about emotions?

We cannot see them at all. It is not possible to view them as different people inside our minds, like in the "Upside down" movie. That is why it is so hard for some children to understand emotions.

Why not take the task literally? Imagine our head is a jar filled with feelings. How would joy look? Anger? Rage? Sadness? Would these emotions be prickly or soft? Would they be dull and unattractive or painted with bright colors?

Let us turn all the feelings churning in our heads into touch. Then we can gather them all together and move them into a big jar of feelings.

What Does One Need To Make A Feeling Jar?

1. Items with different textures and colors: fluffy pompoms, smooth pebbles, prickly cloth, small bundles of wool, etc.
2. A ceramic or glass jar (better something that does not break!).

3. A well – fitted lid.

Additional items: small pieces of paper and a pen; some stickers.

Your feeling jar would look like a big jar filled to the brim with small, safe items with different textures.

There are several ways you can use it:

1. Place the jar into your child's "safe place," so they could play with the items and calm down;

2. Organize a "sort the feelings exercise":
   a. Write down situations on small rectangles of paper. For example, "a friend calls me names at school," "a new girl sat near me and shared her textbook with me," etc.
   b. Place the papers into a "sorting hat."
   c. Let your child take out one task.
   d. Ask him/her to choose items from the jar that would reflect the feelings on the subject.

e. Optionally, place a small sticker to the selected item "Anger," "Resentment," "Joy," etc.

3. Use the feeling jar to help the child explain what he/she feels at present.

   This activity has several benefits:

   – It helps the child relax;
   – It helps the child analyze what he/she feels, to understand his/her emotions;
   – It helps untangle automatic thoughts and feelings;
   – It helps in reaching the root of the anxiety;
   – It helps the child to talk about what he/she has encountered throughout the day.

The activities discussed above also help in one crucial objective – to learn control. By learning to stay in the moment and to analyze your thoughts and feelings, you can control your thoughts – instead of those thoughts controlling you.

Taking Charge Of My Thoughts

The technique of "taking over" the thoughts that plague you are a combination of all the approaches previously described:

1. Find a comfortable space;
2. Take several deep, belly breaths;
3. Focus on the moment – your breathing, the room, your body;
4. Stay in this state for several minutes, give yourself a pause;
5. "Catch" the thoughts that are on your mind;
6. Observe them objectively. Imagine that your thoughts have turned into multi-colored bugs on a tray under a microscope;
7. Do not try to ignore or dismiss what you are thinking – every thought is necessary;
8. Slowly come out of this state. It is possible that you would have some solutions at the end of the exercise, or at least you may have calmed down the never-ending carousel of thoughts.

Remember: dismissing a thought or trying to ban oneself from thinking it would provide it power!

There are other tips to help get some control over your thinking:

1. Distracting yourself with something pleasurable and active: a dance class, a run, a play with friends;
2. Sleeping and eating well – that way your brain would have the energy for solutions!;
3. Regular mindfulness exercises, such as different meditation techniques.

Of course, it is not easy to fully take charge of something that is often automatic. But by helping yourself be strong, active, and mindful, one will be significantly more in charge than before.

The Worry Leap Frog Game

There is another way to work through one's fears. There is a game called worry leap frog game [58]. You would need:

- A self-made "situation pad";
- A small toy frog (or a frog made from plasticine);
- A pen.

The Rules Of The Game

1. Each "Situation pad" is a small pond. There are two sides of the pond: one side is the "Worry path" and the other an "Adventure path."

2. There is a big founding stone where you can write down the main problem at the time. For instance, "I am scared to go out for a walk."

3. Each pair of the stepping stones or leaves in the pong corresponds to a particular area. There are several areas:
   a. **Thoughts** (for example, a "worry thought" – what if I meet bullies there." The "Adventure thought – "What if I meet new friends"?

b. **Feelings** - "I am scared"/ "I am both nervous and excited."

c. **Actions**: "I stay at home/I go out."

d. **Results or outcomes**: ("I am still feeling scared"/ "I had fun (I have made new friends, saw something interesting, etc.").

e. The child can either fill down all the blanks on the stones, or you can fill the blanks for him/her.

Let us start the game! Let us see what path our little froggy would choose.

This game is basically a pros and cons list, but a fun one. There can be many imaginary situations to work through, and maybe, with time, your child would work through real fears. If your child dislikes frogs, replace the animal with someone equally nice and jumpy, like a grasshopper or a rabbit.

Act Positive To Feel Positive

Most children would feel very sad and down by all their

thoughts and fears. When fears consume one, it is tough to "wake up from it." There is no real use or help from telling the kid, "Keep your head up! Get a hold of yourself!" How can one see anything good when the anxiety forms a thick curtain above all the alternative outcomes?!

It is tough to keep a positive mindset in such a situation. Here are a few tips that help one get to a positive place instead of a negative one:

1. Accept one's feelings. I am indeed sad, anxious, and fearful. That is who I am now.

   One of the problems with feeling anxious is that one also feels that he/she is to be blamed or punished for the feelings. When you accept them and know that your closest people accept them too, it removes an enormous burden. It also helps one to be comfortable in one's skin.

2. Set some small, achievable goals and go through them in an orderly manner.

Being able to achieve even small things is an excellent tool against feeling helpless. Instead of thinking "I am bad at everything," one would think "I have completed this today" – a small, but positive thought!

3. Keep a journal.

It can be as simple as writing down all the feelings you had today.

Then one can make a rule to create a small section devoted to the good things that have happened today.

With time, positive experiences may win over the negative ones.

4. Practice positive self-affirmations. For example, a child can say, "I am a superhero who has control

over spiders." Though it may sound stupid, it could help to some extent.

5. Practice saying good things to other people: sincerely thank them, pay compliments, etc. Making people glad may help you feel more joyous, too. Remember Pollyanna!

6. Slowly try to practice optimism. If a child tries to visualize the worst outcome possible, offer him/her also to discuss or visualize better results: "I will be laughed at/I will be accepted into the group or make a friend."

7. Remember that all negative experiences may be another way to gain something important – inspiration, experience, etc. It is hard to think like that and would require some training exercises.

There are multiple ways to help build one's positivity. It is most important to walk through this task with "baby steps," never judging yourself if it does not work out at first. There will be sad days, gloomy days, but there will be lucky days, too.

Talking To Others

One of the dangers of feeling anxious is isolation. The child avoids other people and children, playing alone. This is an ideal ground for negative feelings to grow. Encourage your child to talk. It can be anyone – a trusted adult, a beloved cousin, even a pen pal. Discussing one's thoughts and feelings, things that are important for the child would drive the isolation away, and without it, anxious thoughts would not have much fertilizer to grow.

Being Assertive (Standing Up For Myself)

What is extremely important is to encourage your child to defend himself/herself. People often shame people who are too sad, worried, or scared.

People often are either unaware of the boundaries of

others, or they consciously overstep them. Even if your child has some issues, it does not mean they should be ashamed and feel wrong about them. To help your child be assertive, you must:

1. Show your child that you always have his/her back. Always listen to your child's side of the story. Do not allow other family members to shout at your child for being clumsy, sad, too introverted, etc.

2. Teach your child to assert himself/herself: "Yes, I am clumsy, so what?"; "Yes, I am scared – I have a right to be." It is just as much for the child than for other people. He/she needs to accept the feelings and insecurities.

3. Support them in his/her fight against bullying, injustice, or hurtful comments. Try to think out a strategy on how to counteract them together.

4. It is also good to find a debate class or try practicing debating at home. Being able to construct arguments and counter your opponent with them is a skill akin to a superpower. It would also help with becoming more persuasive and talkative. It is a

useful skill in life even if one does not suffer from anxiety.

5. You can become assertive not only against other people but also against the thoughts that weaken you. To do that, one needs all the coping techniques described above.

One part of being assertive is to find the fears that are the basis of one's anxiety. Here is the necessary step by step strategy to counteract them.

Chapter 10. Actively Fighting Fears Together With Your Child

If you have determined that your child has an anxiety disorder, then it is time to go to battle. You already have some weapons in your arsenal, from possible help from mental health specialists to a toolbox described above. Now you must become your child's closest ally. You would need to plan a strategy that would eventually help conquer the monster.

To fight more effectively, it would be great to make your child a participant. He/she should not remain a sole fortress to be defended.

By allowing the child to understand and participate in his/her treatment, you would help your entire family. It would strengthen your bond and would help the child be more assertive. Not all steps may involve his/her participation, of course. The planning stage may be too complicated for a young child. But it is still good to explain what you are doing and why.

Now, let us go through the steps.

Identify triggers and determine the fear.

We have discussed at length what can cause anxiety and how to cope with an anxious state. But to fight the anxiety head on, we need to identify what triggers the anxiety.

Triggers are a bit different from causes. Usually, triggers are connected to some traumatic or scary events in the past. But some triggers are unexpected, for they are more connected to our physiology than our experiences. Here are some examples of physiological triggers:

1. **Absence of regular meals/access to water.** Low blood sugar and dehydration can lead to many pathological symptoms, such as trembling, nausea, headache, fainting, etc. They can also trigger an anxious state.

Case study. Whenever Cassie skips breakfast, she feels jittery and out of balance. As she often needed to rise early for her cheerleading club, having no breakfast became a norm for her. But she has also noticed that she became more worried, restless, and anxious with time.

When she decided to switch for later practice time and have a regular morning meal, her anxiety subsided.

2. **Lack of sleep.** When the child sleeps irregularly and is overwhelmed with homework, he/she may develop typical anxious symptoms.

Case study 2. Leo had a hard time adapting to a new school. Though the teachers and classmates were amiable, the homework was challenging. He had to stay up almost every night trying to keep up with math assignments and essays. After painstakingly doing his homework for many hours, he had trouble relaxing and falling asleep.

After two months of such a hard schedule, he started feeling worried and anxious about his grades, reports and talking to teachers. He thought he would get to keep up with other students. When Leo decided to drop two of his AP classes and began doing meditation and relaxing exercises, his worries slowly went away.

3. **Medicine.** Some medicines have anxiety development as a side effect. Always check the instructions or discuss them with your GP to ensure they are not the cause of your child's state. Certain groups of medicines can cause anxiety:

   a. steroids,
   b. asthma medicines,
   c. decongestants,
   d. drugs for thyroid problems.

Some addictive substances, such as caffeine, alcohol, and drugs, can also trigger anxiety in users

[60].

Case study 3. Irene had a strange condition – she always had a slight fever. She did not have any other cold symptoms, like a cough or a stuffy nose.

Her GP decided it may be linked to her thyroid and prescribed some new drug agents. But after taking these medicines for two weeks, Irene began feeling anxious and worried. She even started having nightmares. She could not explain why she was feeling this way.

The family moved and changed their GP. After doing some tests, the new doctor determined that Irene's condition had nothing to do with her thyroid, and she stopped taking medicine. In a couple of weeks, when the agents were eliminated from her bloodstream, her anxiety stopped.

4. **Chronic health conditions.** When the child knows he/she is prone to asthma attacks, has difficulty hearing or understanding something, has a disability, anxiety would likely accompany this knowledge.

Case study 4. Steve was hard of hearing. He struggled to hear lessons at school and had a hard time understanding his friend when they were playing at a playground. He began to avoid meeting people and being active in class. He was always afraid he would not be able to hear something important. He slowly began isolating himself.

Then his parents took him to a good audiologist. He was given a better hearing aid, lessons in lip reading, and sign language. He was also taught some tricks that helped him converse better. At his support group, Steve met several friends who had the same problems.

As Steve was starting to meet new friends and has gotten new tools to cope with his disability, he became far less anxious.

Many triggers are social. They revolve around events and people in the child's life.

a. **Social situations or specific places.** A traumatic event – bullying, embarrassment, or a failed grade - can affect the child to such an extent that all conditions like the first traumatic event can become triggers. A particular place can also become a trigger, too: if the child witnessed something scary in the forest, he/she would be scared of any wooded areas in the future.

Case Study 5. There was this place not far from Ivy's home. It was a beautiful meadow with flowers and butterflies. But once, Ivy was attacked by a big dog that was let loose by its owner. Ivy was bitten and had to have stitches and several painkiller shots.

After that experience, she began avoiding this meadow and, though it was on her way to school, she preferred to choose routes as far from the place as possible. She began to dislike other open spaces, too. She hated dog parks with a passion, for example.

Because of this, she was consistently late to school and also skipped some events with her friends that took place in similar places.

But then Ivy thought that some events in her past should not control her. She decided to face her fear of dogs. After exposure therapy, she was not afraid of meadows any more. Even better - she has gotten a Springer spaniel!

b. **Personal loss**.

A loss of someone dear to the child is a cause for grief. But this is also a cause for anxiety. If the child used to rely on the person he/she has lost, anxiety is the next logical stage.

Case study 6. John used to have a dear friend, Robin. He was his best friend. Robin and John used to sit together, do homework together, and plan games. Robin was far more outgoing than John.

One day, Robin's parents were forced to move away to another country. Now, Robin was extremely far away. The Internet connection there was unstable, and the letters took a long time to arrive. John was very sad. He also began to feel incredibly isolated. He began to fear the children would not be playing with him now, as his fun friend was now gone.

Then, John discovered desktop games. They were more suitable for him than running and jumping games his schoolmates preferred. He also found a club where kids developed their desktop games, painting and cutting out figurines for them. The club was a good fit for him.

John became much happier. He also sent a self-made desktop game for Robin as a Christmas present.

As you can see from the case studies, each trigger may require its solution. So it is important to find the correct "button" that switches the anxiety in your child. It is much easier to develop a master plan when you know the enemy.

Here are some tips that will help you with finding the right triggers:

1. **Ask your child to start a journal.** By writing one's experiences, it would be easier to pinpoint the event, place, or action that is linked to feeling worried and scared. While you should not read the journal, you can discuss the events in some fashion.

2. **Therapy.** By talking with a professional counselor, the child may suddenly discover the cause of the problems he/she is experiencing.

3. **Playing with the feeling jar.** The technique described above may be a great way to realize the cause of the fear by discussing what he/she feels about people, situations, and places and helping them choose the proper emotions.

4. **Make a diary of observations yourself.** If your child cannot yet write or does not like to, note everything you observe. Compare the behavior before and after your child has developed anxiety. What was new in his/her life? New people? New experiences? A new prescription? Sudden loss of someone or something?

5. **Eliminate some obvious triggers.** Ensure that your child has enough food and water at all times. Help him/her organize the routine so there would be no less than eight hours of undisturbed sleep. Review the instructions for all the medicines that you must give.

It may also be a good idea to replace strong tea blends with milder ones or switch to herbal teas. In short, do everything to eliminate the possible physiological triggers.

Now, when we have discovered more about fears and triggers that your child has, it is time to counteract their influence.

How to Stop Feeding Your Child's Fear

Sometimes, our words and actions, even if they are meant kindly, stoke the fire of fears. Here are some things you absolutely must avoid not to feed your child's insecurities and fears:

1. **Do not support the child's avoidance behavior**.

   It does not mean that you have to force him/her to go outside or participate in something.

Instead, gently encourage them to overcome this fear and show that it is okay to be outside sometimes.

2. **Do not shame or laugh at him/her for their fears.**

Shaming a person is not "tough love." Strictly speaking, it is not loved at all. Such behavior is hurtful and feeds the same avoidance loop we discussed earlier.

3. **Do not be overprotective and overly accommodating.**

For example, if the child has separation anxiety, show that you would always be there if needed. It shouldn't mean that you would stay at home always and avoid social activities or going out to make the child feel better.

4. **Do not be repetitive and over-the-top with reassurances.**

Showing support and love are okay and reasonable, but when you continuously repeat the same thing, it may indicate to the child that you are worried and insecure.

5. **Do not discuss his/her problems with strangers (unless it is a therapist and your child permits this).**

By discussing your child's problems with strangers, you are violating your child's privacy and damage his/her self-respect. Always show him/her consideration and support in public instead.

6. **Do not discourage him/her from trying something new or getting out of the comfort zone.**

Even if you are afraid of your child getting hurt, it is still better than coddling them too much and discouraging them. If you are worried about a child's safety, take some measures for protection.

7. **Do not lie to your child or evade uncomfortable subjects.**

As mentioned earlier, you should allow your child to know about their condition. If your child has a disorder, he/she must be the first to understand and know all about the disorder.

The same can be said for traumatic subjects, such as the loss of a family member or an unpleasant event in the family. Your child does not need to take responsibility for adult problems, but they need to understand these subjects exist.

In short, show your child support and understanding. Also, remember that your child follows your example in most things – so if you are anxious yourself, show them there are healthy and constructive ways to deal with uncomfortable subjects. Practice what you preach.

How to Stop Your Child from Feeding Their

Fear

You may be doing your best to create a supportive atmosphere for your child, but you cannot get into his/her head and stop their thoughts. Instead, give them instruments for coping with fears and teach them in their use.

1. Teach them breathing exercises that would help with eliminating anxious feelings: deep breathing, counting, short meditations;
2. Encourage him/her to talk about how he/she feels with someone trustworthy;
3. Encourage him/her in writing a journal that would help him/her analyze their actions and feelings;
4. Show him/her your acceptance so the child would be able to accept themselves;
5. Create spaces for the child to relax and play and encourage their use;
6. Teach him/her assertiveness. It is good to enroll him/her in some special classes such as martial arts, yoga, arts, etc. New skills would help your child feel significantly better about everything;

7. Try to show your child positive examples and outcomes for the things he/she fears;

To stop feeding his/her fear, your child needs to stop feeling helpless. Instead of fears, one needs to learn about feeding empowerment instead.

What is empowerment? Empowerment means getting instruments and power to deal with the problems presented. By helping your child to understand his/her condition and providing tools, you stop the helplessness your child feels. In other words, empowerment is the opposite of helplessness. When the child knows they can deal with his/her issues, even in some small way, the feelings would slowly change for the better.

Besides the general tools against anxiety, there should be some specific ones. As we already know, children have different fears. And each anxiety disorder is a little different because a different fear triggers it.

We can truly subdue our fear only if we face the fear. That is why exposure therapy – learning to face our fears head-on – is such an important part of treating any anxiety.

Plan Development for Exposures

One of the most effective methods for counteracting anxiety is the so-called exposure therapy. The main idea behind the treatment is like allergy therapy.

To become less sensitive to an allergen, one needs to be exposed to a minimal amount.

With time, this amount can be increased. This type of therapy helps build a tolerance to the allergen. If the treatment is successful, in a few months the patient may not experience hay fever or a rash in response to flower pollen, for instance.

The same principle can work for fear. Encountering something one is afraid of (an animal, a place, etc.) in a safe, controlled setting can help the patient slowly get used to the feared object or situation [60].

The key to successful exposure therapy lies in carrying it out slowly and systematically. If a child is forced to face something scary immediately, this will not result in desensitization. Instead, it could cause further trauma.

Would you throw your child into the sea to teach swimming? The child may very well drown! Treat exposure therapy in the same way you would plan swimming lessons. Psychological exposure treatments are usually developed together with professional therapists and counselors that specialize in cognitive behavior therapy, but you can make a general plan yourself and discuss it with a professional:

1. **Identify the triggers of a particular fear**

You already know that the question of triggers is complex. When planning for exposure therapy, we would assume that no physiological triggers are present. Work with places, objects, and animals.

2. **Make a ranking sheet.**
   Work together with the child. Make a list of unpleasant, fearful thinks. Ask the child to rank the fears from 1 to 10, where 1 is the scariest, and 10 is the least scary. You can also discuss each fear for a while to get a better understanding.

3. **Decide on the type of exposure that is most suitable**.
   There are several types of exposure:
   - **Interceptive exposure**
     This is exposure through touch. For example, frogs and snakes are quite unpleasant to the touch. This can be used in the course of the treatment;

   - **Visual exposure**

Using scary images or portraits of things/animals/people connected with the fear;

- **Imaginative exposure**
  In imaginative exposure, the therapist or the counselor uses role-playing games and scenarios of possible situations to help the patient find the right responses.

- **In vivo exposure**
  This type of exposure is the strongest in terms of impact. It involves a direct encounter with the object of fear.

Each type of fear/anxiety disorder would need its mode of exposure. For example, social anxiety would probably require imaginative exposure, while specific phobias such as fears of heights or dogs would require in vivo exposure.

4. **Organize a safe place for exposures**.

Learning swimming would require a swimming pool and safety tools. Exposure therapy should take place in a setting where the child feels equally safe: the workplace of the therapist, a natural setting, a favorite room at home.

5. **Make a roadmap for fear exposure to check all the milestones along the road.**

    The roadmap should contain the following:

    a. The fear that you would need to eliminate;

    b. Possible triggers/reasons for it;

    c. Steps for exposure therapy;

    d. Milestones: a child can look at a photo of a scary animal or object; the child can look at the real object/animal; the child can touch/interact with it; the child does not feel fear anymore.

6. **Ensure that the exposure therapy takes place together with a trustworthy, supportive adult, or a therapist.**

    Do not conduct exposure therapy yourself. In many cases, additional fears, worries, or traumatic events may surface, and the counselor would work with them. Moreover, a mistake in exposure therapy can lead to progressive worsening of the child's condition.

Find exposures that work.

Even with the right exposure, therapy may take considerable time. According to statistics [61], the treatment of specific phobias may take a couple of months.

More complex conditions, such as social anxiety may take up to a year.

There are several important things one must pay attention to when undergoing exposure therapy:

- Exposure therapy must proceed slowly, in small doses;

- Exposures must be done not only in the presence of the specialist/adult but also by the child on their own (for example, exercises)
- The types of exposures chosen must work.

How to determine if the exposure works as expected:

1. **Use the so-called worry scale/subjective units of distress scale.**

   After the exposure session, offer the child to range their feelings. Have they felt no anxiety (0) or were they completely terrified (100)? Or was it something in between?

2. **Ask the child how severe was the child's reaction to the exposure.**

   For example, did the child shake with fear after seeing a spider (or a photo/video of one)?

3. **Evaluate if the child can sit through the session.**

   If the mode of exposure is incorrectly chosen, the child may bolt away immediately. If the exposure chosen is not strong enough, the child would be bored at the sessions. The exposure must elicit a reaction that is neither too strong nor too weak.

To understand whether the exposure works or not, document every session. It is necessary to place the process in perspective and understand whether there were shifts in behavior compared to the start of the therapy.

If the child cannot tolerate the exposure at all or feels completely terrified, then one needs to change the exposure amount. For example, one can exchange a live spider for a drawing of one or decrease the time of exposure.

If the exposure does not induce any negative reaction, it may also not be working.

For example, imagine that the child works calmly

through role-plays of social situations, but is still afraid of meeting people in a real setting. This would mean that the plays were chosen wrong and do not involve the real fear or trigger.

We cannot expect anxiety to disappear overnight after therapy. The progress may be slow, and the child may relapse. That is why it is important to give credit where credit is due – recognize achievement, no matter how small. It is also important to provide measures against possible relapses.

Recognize progress and prevent relapse.

In the previous chapter, we had already discussed some instruments that would help determine if there is progress in our fight against anxiety:

1. **Worry scale.**
   With the help of the worry scale, you can evaluate how your child feels. You could use it before and after the therapy sessions. It is also good to make a more comprehensive scale or questionnaire where

the child would rate how he/she now feels in different trigger situations and their overall sense of well-being.

2. **Observe the symptoms.**

   Make a list of symptoms of your child's disorder. Take note if they have changed for the better. Has your child started eating and sleeping better? Has he/she begun to go out more, meeting friends? Have some or all the disruptive behaviors stopped? Are there any more nightmares? Document all progress for each symptom group.

3. **Discussion time.**

   Try to organize family time and discussions to provide your child with an opportunity to discuss his/her thoughts and feelings. It can be a game or debate, so the child would not feel pressured. It would also be useful to introduce a family tradition of discussing how the day has passed for each family member. This would help your child to open up and feel equal.

4. **Make a success wall.**

   Put a billboard or a desk devoted to all your child's successes. Each good thing, however small, must be noted. For example, going to a party or visiting an insect exhibit. All notes should be put together with your child. It would be good to select a type of token for this activity.

One of the most dangerous things about anxiety is that it can often return. A new stressful event, an unkind neighbor or a child may undo all the careful work you have completed. To prevent relapses, or at least minimize the damage, you must build your child's resilience.

According to Psychology Today, resilience is a quality that allows us to recover from traumatic events [61]. For children, it also means to be able to find tools and people that would help them weather the storms that come their way. To make your child more resilient, you should:

1. **Remind him/her about your acceptance.**
   Always let your children know that there is a safe and supportive place at home;

2. **Provide the child with a list of techniques and a box of simple tools for relaxation and de-stressing.**
   The child should always have on hand his/her meditation CDs, stress balls, bubble bottles, soft toys, favorite music, painting books, and other helpful things.

3. **A child needs energy to bounce back.**
   Proper nutrition and enough sleep can go a long way in making your child mentally stronger. Doing even the simplest of sports can also improve your child's mood and outlook significantly.

4. **Practice positive thinking yourself and teach your child the same.**

Failures should be treated as learning experiences, not soul-crushing blows. If you encounter problems, show your child that you have ways to learn from them and cope. Support him/her when they are sad, but also teach them how to find a grain of goodness everywhere.

5. **Find relaxing, enjoyable activities together with your child.**
Your child must have an activity that would bring him/her enjoyment. It can be anything from gaming to carving.

Respect the time your child assigns to this activity. There needs to be some refuge, an outlet for both creativity and frustrations. It would be even better if the activity is social and involves other family members or friends.

6. **The child needs to have a confidante.**
It may not always be you, as a parent or guardian. It could be a relative or a good friend. In extreme

cases, there should always be a therapist to provide some emotional support.

Chapter 11. Making A Step By Step Plan

While we discuss various strategies aimed at winning over anxiety, we need to acknowledge a sad truth. Parents can also feel anxious and scared when they are faced with those new, disruptive behaviors in their child. But we now know one of the major causes of anxiety – feeling helpless.

The opposite of this feeling, as we also know, is empowerment and control. And this control is ours for the taking.

Of course, we cannot get into the heads of our children. We cannot win over all the bullies or chase away all the spiders. But we can plant a strategy that would help both parents and the child deal with the disorder. This strategy would have to be as thorough as possible and take into account every contingency. This way, with this enormous list of what to do and when we would feel much better. And we would know what to do!

Step 1. Observation.

So, your child was issued a diagnosis: anxiety disorder. Instead of feeling overwhelmed, let us sit down and observe. Note all the symptoms your child is having. Also, note when those symptoms can be seen. For example, when does your child have panic attacks? How often does your child have nightmares? For how long has your child started to stay all the time indoors?

Step 2. Theory.

Note all new events that may have happened related to your child's condition. Try to remember everything: a new, nasty uncle at your friend's wedding; a recent cockroach invasion; a new, unusual pupil at school. You never know what the trigger was.

Step 3. Medical procedures

Go to your GP/family doctor and for blood tests: sometimes anxiety is a symptom of a treatable, physiological problem such as a thyroid disorder. Also, inspect all the recently prescribed medicines. Eliminate any possible addiction or poisoning.

Step 4. Recognizance

Think about possible influences on your child. Has he/she been bullied? Does he/she have some toxic friends? Are there problems at kindergarten or school? Talk with your child's teachers and trainers. It would also be useful to talk to children in the playground. Observe if there are some people, family or otherwise, that your child actively avoids and dislikes. Sometimes a family member may instill anxiety and low self-esteem in the child because of the way he/she was raised in the past.

Step 5. Gather further intelligence.

If an illness as a cause is excluded, make an appointment with a counselor and discuss the situation. What are the possible lines of treatments available? Would exposure therapy help? Would there be a need to take medicine?

Step 6. Active preparation.

Change the environment in your home if you can. Redecorate your child's room. Try to create safe places and nooks throughout the house and outside in the garden. Buy or create feeling jars and stress balls. Compose meditation CDs. Gather all the anti-anxiety weaponry available.

Step 7. Repair communication lines.

Do your best to reconnect with your child. Take an interest in their hobbies and worries. Do not demand answers immediately. Show him/her that you can be trusted and you will wait for the time he/she will be ready to confide in you. Invent some games like the leaping frog game to discuss the child's problems in some fashion.

Step 8. Offensive maneuvers

If you have managed to identify the triggers and causes of your child's condition, discuss possible therapy approaches with the specialist again.

Everyone involved - you, your therapist, and your child - would need journals to track the progress of the treatment. Hang up the success board on the wall of the child's room. The battle is starting in earnest.

Step 9. Good training is worth half of the battle.

Before teaching your child the new techniques, learn meditation, deep breathing, and relaxation yourself first. Choose methods most suitable for your child's age and temperament. Take all the steps described above to build resilience and help decrease the fears in your child.

Step 10. Engage in everything.

Never cease to observe the progress of the therapy and

new lines of treatment. Also, be vigilant about new events in the child's life.

The changes at school and in your neighborhood may have both positive and negative consequences. While your child may have the tools for resilience building, it would always pay to prevent the negative influence instead of dealing with the aftermath.

Step 11. Try something new.

Search for new clubs, interests, and hobbies. Find new activities. Try to help your child see good things in everyday life. Invent new positive experiences – from new food flavors to small adventures outside and inside.

Step 12. Build your child's self-esteem.

By talking with your child and their closest circle, try to identify areas he/she excels. Encourage those activities, even if you do not understand.

Step 13. Remember about safety.

Your child needs to know ways to protect himself/herself from dangers their condition may involve.

For example, he/she needs to have a badge with identification in case of a panic attack or a seizure. They would also need to have a mobile phone on hand if something scares him/her and would need to get home. There should always be a trusted person nearby if you need to go somewhere or the child goes on a trip or a visit.

Step 14. Join a parent's club.

People often misunderstand mental illness. Also, they do not understand what parents of children that suffer from those conditions are undergoing. Besides consulting a therapist, try to find parents that have children with similar problems. Meeting with them and discussing different cases may provide you with new insights and information. Which is even more important – you would find support and understanding that you need.

It is crucial to remember that anxiety is a very manipulative enemy. You can always expect that there will be relapses, and sometimes you would feel as if you go one step forward and two steps back. Still, even the most severe case of anxiety can be controlled and overcome. Using the techniques and approaches suggested here, you can assist your child win this battle.

Conclusion

Fighting anxiety is not easy. It is a condition that affects us all. We worry about our loved ones, our health, our finances. Anxiety has multiple causes. Our genes, the makeup of our brains and our overall health have significant control over our thoughts and feelings. So do other external factors, such as attitudes of other people among us. The combination of those factors can be hard to overcome for young children. They have not yet built their emotional intelligence, and they have a hard time understanding themselves.

That is why our help in deciphering this complex world is so important. This book is aimed to help you with control over your fears and feelings. Here, we did our best to provide you with relevant scientific information on mechanisms and approaches to anxiety. You can now see that an anxiety disorder can be partially controlled with simple and effective methods. Hopefully, the information described here will help you understand anxiety disorders better.

There is one more important point to remember: while family situation and lifestyle changes may help, only a certified therapist can issue a conclusive diagnosis and plan treatment. If you do not trust your current doctor, try to find another one, but do not medicate or treat your child without a specialist's supervision!

References

1. Hill, C. et al., (December, 2016). Anxiety disorders in children and adolescents. Pediatric and Child Health, 26 (12), 548-33

2. Anxiety and depression in adolescence (n.d.). Child Mind Institute. Retrieved June 14, 2019 from: https://childmind.org/report/2017-childrens-mental-health-report/anxiety-depression-adolescence/#_ftn1

3. American Psychiatric Association (2000). Diagnostic and Statistical Manual for Mental Disorders, Fourth Edition, Text Revision (4th edition). Washington, DC: American Psychiatric Association.

4. Asbahr, F. R. (April, 2004). Anxiety disorders in childhood and adolescence: clinical and neurobiological aspects. J. Pediatr. (Rio J.), V. 80 (2), Suppl. 0 Porto Alegre

5. Cummings, C. M. et al. (May, 2014). Comorbidity of Anxiety and Depression in Children and Adolescents: 20 Years After. Psych. Bull. 140 (3), 816-845

6. Wolk, C. B., and R. S. Beidas (May 1, 2016). Cognitive-Behavioral Therapy for Child Anxiety Confers Long-Term Protection From Suicidality. J. Am. Acad. Child. Adolesc. Psychiatry., 54(3), 175-179

7. Thompson-Hollands, J. et al. (December, 16, 2014). Parental accommodation of child anxiety and related symptoms: Range, impact, and correlates. J. Anxiety Disord., 28(8), 765-773

8. Bhatt, N. V. et al. (March, 27, 2019). Anxiety disorders. Retrieved June 14, 2019 from: https://emedicine.medscape.com/article/286227-overview

9. Daniel Zwillenberg PsyD. (19 April 2018). Anxiety and Panic attacks: your questions answered. ABC-CLIO, 160 p.

10. Ollendick, T. H., et al. (January 1991). Fears in British Children and Their Relationship to Manifest Anxiety and Depression. The Journal of Child Psychology and Psychiatry, V. 32, Issue 2, 321-331.

11. Bagnell, A. L. (October 2011). Anxiety and separation disorders. Pediatrics in Review, 32(10), 440-446

12. Beesdo, K. et al. (September 2009). Anxiety and Anxiety Disorders in Children and Adolescents: Developmental Issues and Implications for DSM-V. Psychiatr.Clin. North. Am., 32(3), 483-524.

13. Strawn, J. R, (September 1, 2014). Neurobiology of pediatric anxiety. Curr. Behav.Neur. Rep., 1(3), 154-160.

14. Wright, A. (n.d.) Chapter 6: Limbic System: Amygdala. Neuroscience online. Retrieved June 14, 2019 from: https://nba.uth.tmc.edu/neuroscience/m/index.htm

15. Martin, E. I. et al. (September 2009). The Neurobiology of Anxiety Disorders: Brain Imaging, Genetics, and Psychoneuroendocrinology. Psych. Clin. North. Am. 32(3), 549-575

16. Engel, K et al. (2009). Neuroimaging in anxiety disorders. J Neural Transm. (116), 703–716.

17. Kilts, C. D. (October 2006). The neural correlates of social anxiety disorder and response to pharmacotherapy. Neuropsychoparmacology. 31(10), 2243-53

18. Patriquin, M. A., and M. J. Sanjay (2017). The Neurobiological Mechanisms of Generalized

Anxiety Disorder and Chronic Stress. Chronic Stress (Thousand Oaks), Jan-Dec., 1.

19. Guyer, A. E. et al. (November, 2008). Amygdala and ventrolateral prefrontal cortex function during anticipated peer evaluation in pediatric social anxiety. Arc. Gen. Psychiatry. 65 (11), 1303-12

20. Borrow, et al. (2016). Neuroendocrine regulation of anxiety: Beyond the hypothalamic-pituitary axis. Journal of neuroendocrinology, 28 (7). doi: 10.1111/jne.12403.

21. Li, X., Sundquist J., Sundquist K. (2008). Age-specific familial risks of anxiety. A nation-wide epidemiological study from Sweden. Eur. Arch. Neurosc., 258(7), 441-5

22. Smith, D. J. et al. (June 2016). Genome-wide analysis of over 106 000 individuals identifies 9 neuroticism-associated loci. Mol. Psychiatry, 21(6), 749-57.

23. Gottschalk, M. D. (June 2017). Genetics of generalized anxiety disorder and related traits. Dialogues Clin. Neurosci. 19(2), 159-168.

24. Weinstock, L. M., Whisman M. A. (February 2006). Neuroticism as a common feature of the depressive and anxiety disorders: a test of the revised integrative hierarchical model in a national sample. J. Abnorm. Psych. 115 (1), 68-74

25. Fox, A. S. et al. (August 2018). Functional Connectivity within the Primate Extended Amygdala Is Heritable and Associated with Early-Life Anxious Temperament. J. Neurosci. 38 (35), 7611-7621

26. Henriques, G. (February, 26. 2017). Trait neuroticism and depressive and anxiety disorders. Psychology Today. Retrieved June 14, 2019 from: https://www.psychologytoday.com/us/blog/theor

y-knowledge/201702/trait-neuroticism-and-depressive-and-anxiety-disorders

27.   Britton, J. C. et al. (January, 2011). Development of anxiety: the role of threat appraisal and fear learning. Depress. Anxiety, 28(1) 5-17.

28.   Jacowski, M. D. et al. (n.d.). Paired association and classical conditioning. Gracepointwellness.org. Retrieved   May   23,   2019   from: https://www.gracepointwellness.org/1-anxiety-disorders/article/38478-paired-association-and-classical-conditioning

29.   Duby, K. et al. (May, 2008). Maternal modeling and the acquisition of fear and avoidance in toddlers: influence of stimulus preparedness and child temperament. J. Abnorm. Child. Psychol., 36(4), 499-512.

30.   Broeren, S. et al. (2011). They are afraid of the animal, so therefore I am too: Influence of peer

modeling on fear beliefs and approach-avoidance behaviors towards animals in typically developing children. Behaviour Research and Therapy, 49, 50-57.

31. Nathan, P. et al. (2003). Module 3. The thinking-feeling connection. Back from the Bluez. Perth, Western Australia: Centre for Clinical Interventions.

32. Mann, D. (n.d.) 9 Steps to End Chronic Worrying. Health and Balance Home. WebMD. Retrieved June 10, 2019 from: https://www.webmd.com/balance/features/9-steps-to-end-chronic-worrying#1

33. Bourdon, J. L. et al. (2019) The genetic and environmental relationship between childhood behavioral inhibition and preadolescent anxiety. Twin.Res. Hum. Genetics, 22 (1), 48-55.

34. Cooper-Vince, C. et al. (2014). Maternal intrusiveness, family financial means, and anxiety across childhood in a large multiphase sample of community youth. J. Abnorm. Child. Psychol., 42 (3), 429-438.

35. Alvares-Garcia, D. et al. (13 September 2016). Parenting Style Dimensions As Predictors for Adolescents Antisocial Behavior. Frontiers in Psychology. Retrieved June 17, 2019 from https://www.frontiersin.org/articles/10.3389/fpsyg.2016.01383/full

36. Garcia, F. and Gracia E. (Spring 2009) Is always authoritative the optimum parenting style? Evidence from Spanish families. Adolescence, 44 (173), 101-31.

37. Rymanowich, K. (May 4, 2017). Children and empathy: Kindness. Michigan State University. MSU extension. Retrieved June 16, 2019 from:

https://www.canr.msu.edu/news/children_and_e
mpathy_kindness

38.   Stuart, A. Childhood fears and worries. WebMD.
Retrieved   June   14,   2019   from:
https://www.webmd.com/parenting/features/chil
dhood-fears-anxieties#1

39.   Colonessi, K. et al. (April, 2014). Positive and
negative expressions of shyness in toddlers: are
they related to anxiety in the same way? J. Pers.
Soc. Psychol. 106(4), 624-37.

40.   Colonessi, K. et al. (2017). Social Anxiety
Symptoms in Young Children: Investigating the
Interplay of Theory of Mind and Expressions of
Shyness J. Abnorm. Child Psychol. 45(5), 997-1011.

41.15 Insightful quesions to identify your fears (n.d.).
Followyourownrhythm.com. Retrieved June 14,
2019   from:
https://www.followyourownrhythm.com/blog-

1/2018/10/15/how-to-identify-your-fears-15-insightful-questions

42.   Matheis, L. (March 14, 2016). Identifying signs of anxiety in children. Anxiety. Org. Retrieved June 14, 2019 from: https://www.anxiety.org/causes-and-symptoms-of-anxiety-in-children

43.   Hoffman, G. (July 8, 2018) Using Mindfulness to treat Anxiety. Psych Central. Retrieved June 14, 2019 from: https://psychcentral.com/blog/using-mindfulness-to-treat-anxiety-disorders/

44.   Scott, E. (August 1, 2018). Body scan meditation. Verywellmind. Retrieved June 14, 2019 from: https://www.verywellmind.com/body-scan-meditation-why-and-how-3144782

45.   Anxiety Canada (n.d.). How to do progressive muscle relaxation. Retrieved June 14, 2019 from: https://www.anxietycanada.com/sites/default/files/MuscleRelaxation.pdf

46.   Anxiety in Adults (n.d.). Anxiety Canada. Retrieved June 24, 2019 from: https://anxietycanada.com/learn-about-anxiety/anxiety-in-adults/

47.   Body – focused repetitive behaviors (n. d.) Anxiety Canada. Retrieved June 24, 2019 from: https://anxietycanada.com/disorders/body-focused-repetitive-behaviours/

48.   Eilam, D. et al. (March 2011). Threat detection: Behavioral practices in animals and humans. Neuroscience and Biobehavioral Reviews, 35 (4), 999-1006;

49.   Gezginci, E. et al (2018). Three Distraction Methods for Pain Reduction During Cystoscopy: A Randomized Controlled Trial Evaluating the Effects on Pain, Anxiety, and Satisfaction. J. Endourology, 32 (11), 1078-1094.

50. Hudson, et al. (November 2015) Randomized controlled trial to compare the effect of simple distraction interventions on pain and anxiety experienced during conscious surgery. European Journal of Pain, 19(10), 1447-1455.

51. Stalvey, S. and H. Brasell (2006). Using Stress Balls to Focus the Attention of Sixth-Grade Learners. Journal of At-risk Issues, 12(2), 7-16.

52. Murphy, L. (June 3, 2019). How to make a stress ball. The Spruce Crafts. Retrieved June, 24 from: https://www.thesprucecrafts.com/how-to-make-a-stress-ball-1244219

53. Riley-Romedico, V. A. et al. (March 2018). The Effects of Fidget Spinners and Stress Balls on Attention in College Students. Poster. Annual Meeting of the Southeastern Psychological Association. Charleston, SC.

54. Chen, K. W. et al. (July 2012). Meditative Therapies for Reducing Anxiety: A Systematic Review and Meta-analysis of Randomized Controlled Trials. Depress. Anxiety, 29(7), 545-562.

55. Zeidan, F. et al. (June 2014). Neural correlates of mindfulness meditation-related anxiety relief. Soc. Cogn.Affect. Neurosci., 9(6), 751-759.

56. Seo, H.-J. Et al. (2007). The Effect of Oxygen Inhalation on Cognitive Function and EEG in Healthy Adults. Clinical psychopharmacology and neuroscience. 5(1), 25-30.

57. Breath and the Brain. Brainworks: train your mind. Retrieved 1 July, 2019, from: https://brainworksneurotherapy.com/breath-and-brain

58. Alter, R. and Crystal Clarke. (2016) The Anxiety workbook for kids: Take charge of fears and worries using the gift of imagination. Instant Help,

Workbook edition. 136 pages. ISBN-13: 978-1626254770

59.   RelayHealth (2014) Substance –induced anxiety disorder. Summit medical group. Retrieved July, 12 , 2019, from: https://www.summitmedicalgroup.com/library/adult_health/bha_substance_induced_anxiety_disorder/

60.   Blakey, S. M., and B. J. Deacon (January 2015). Exposure treatment. In: Phobias: The Psychology of Irrational Fear, an Encyclopedia. ABC-CLIO; Ed.: I. Milosevic, R. McCabe, pp.140-143

61. Resilience. Psychology today. Retrieved August 17,2019 from: https://www.psychologytoday.com/us/basics/resilience

Anxiety Workbook For Kids

Proven Tools To Cure Your Kids Paralyzing Fear

By

Lawrence Conley

Introduction

Anxiety comes in many different forms and is more common than one may think. About 40 million people in the United States are affected by anxiety. These issues are, of course, not just specific to adults, as about eight percent of children and teens experience an anxiety disorder, and most of them develop symptoms before they turn 21. [22]

Many children suffer from some form of an anxiety disorder, and as a parent, you may recognize the signs but are not sure of what to do. Any parent would want their child to have the best life possible, and when anxiety disorders prevent your child from going to school, making friends and just being a kid, then the parent can feel helpless when they are not sure what to do about their child's problem.

It is easy to feel helpless in such a situation, but there is a solution. In today's day and age, anxiety disorders are more widely recognized and understood than ever before. Numerous studies have been done about the causes of anxiety, the different types of anxiety and methods for recovery and coping mechanisms. Some of these solutions that can help your child include smart talk, calming skills, and processing skills.

As a researcher who has spent years exploring the meaning of different types of anxiety, and having experienced a few of them firsthand, I am here to help you navigate the world of childhood anxiety and its solutions.

The world of anxiety is vast and can sometimes seem a little overwhelming and confusing. But, taking it one topic at a time and identifying what works for you can bring about an immense sense of relief. After implementing some of the strategies in this book, you and your child's life will seem much calmer, much more comfortable, and more fun.

The strategies for dealing with anxiety outlined in this

book have been thoroughly studied by top psychologists, universities and more who have been active in interacting with people who struggle with anxiety firsthand and have seen results in their practices and studies.

I cannot promise you that every single thing discussed in this book will work for you, but what I can promise is that it will give you a jumping-off point and some more clarity as to what anxiety is and where to go from there.

You may be skeptical, and you may wonder if this is the right place to look. But if you don't take a look and give it a try, you will never know if it will work. After all, your child is your primary concern, and it is never too soon to start helping to improve their lives.

So be open-minded as you read ahead. The time to help your child have a better life is now.

What Is Anxiety?

The Definition Of Anxiety

Throughout the United States, 18 percent of the population experiences some form of anxiety disorder in any given year. On a global level, 1 in 13 people around the world suffer from an anxiety disorder, but even though anxiety disorders are so prevalent in our society, only one-third of people who suffer seek treatment. [22]

This is not just an issue that affects adults. Studies report that anxiety disorders are the most frequently diagnosed class of disorders among adolescents and children. What's more, is that those anxiety problems affect 10 to 20 percent of school-age children. [22]

At its most basic level, the American Psychological Association defines anxiety as "an emotion characterized by feelings of tension, worried thoughts and physical changes like increased blood pressure."

With that, people with anxiety disorders will tend to experience recurring thoughts or concerns, will avoid certain situations out of worry, and may also experience physical symptoms that include sweating, trembling, dizziness or a rapid heartbeat.

In understanding anxiety disorders, it is essential to note that there is basic, everyday anxiety, and then there are anxiety disorders. [22]

Anxiety disorders differ from anxiety as they refer to specific psychiatric disorders that involve extreme worry and fear.

Types Of Anxiety Disorders

- **Generalized Anxiety Disorder (GAD):**
  Generalized Anxiety Disorder is described as persistent and excessive worry about a number of things. These include anticipating disaster and worrying about things such as money, health,

family, work, and more, finding it difficult to control their worry and worrying more than is necessary or even when there is no reason to worry at all. People who suffer from GAD do not know how to control this worry cycle, and just thinking about getting through the next day produces anxiety for them. [22]

The situation becomes GAD instead of everyday worries about day-to-day life when a person finds it difficult to control their concerns on more days than not, and the problems persist for more than six months. The symptoms of GAD include feeling nervous, irritable or on edge, increased/rising heart rate, breathing rapidly, sweating and trembling, feeling weak or tired, difficulty concentrating and having trouble sleeping with such symptoms being constant.

On average, 6.1 percent of the population in the United States, or 6.8 million adults, suffer from

GAD with women being more likely to be affected than men. The disorder can begin at any point in life, with childhood being the most high-risk time for it to develop. [22]

- **Panic Disorder and Panic Attacks:**

Panic Disorder is when people experience and sometimes out-of-nowhere panic attacks, also known as anxiety attacks, characterized by at least four symptoms that include palpitations, pounding heart or accelerated heart rate, sweating, trembling or shaking, shortness of breath, feelings of choking, chest pain, nausea or abdominal distress and feeling dizzy, unsteady, light-headed or faint. People who have panic disorder are often preoccupied with the fear of having another attack.

About 2-3 percent of Americans have panic disorder. While it is not very common in people under the age of 20, it is possible for children to experience panic attacks and be diagnosed with panic disorder and many children do experience panic-like symptoms, also called "fearful spells." This disorder can very much interfere with daily life causing people to be afraid of and avoid situations where they fear they might have a panic attack. It becomes especially bad when people also have agoraphobia or the fear of being overwhelmed by anxiety and not being able to escape. [22]

- **Social Anxiety Disorder:**

Social Anxiety Disorder is defined as "intense anxiety or fear of being judged, negatively evaluated or rejected in a social or performance situation." People with this disorder worry about visibly appearing as anxious as they feel and in turn be viewed as awkward, annoying, or stupid. People with Social Anxiety Disorder will avoid social or performance situations because of this and experience immense anxiety and stress when a social situation cannot be avoided. [8]

About 15 million Americans face Social Anxiety Disorder, and it is the second most common anxiety disorder next to specific phobias. On average, people begin to experience the disorder around their teenage years. Social Anxiety Disorder is rarely diagnosed in childhood. Although people report being shy as children, the two are not necessarily the same thing as Social Anxiety Disorder takes on more extreme symptoms.

The physical symptoms of Social Anxiety Disorder can also include rapid heart rate, nausea, and sweating. People can even experience full-blown attacks when confronting what they fear because of the disorder. Additionally, they recognize that their fear is irrational and often feel helpless. It can wreak havoc on a person's social life, as it can cause people to turn down job opportunities, disrupt day-to-day life, and make it difficult to finish school or experience friendships or relationships. [22]

- **Specific Phobias:**

  The number one diagnosed anxiety disorder, Specific Phobias, are strong, irrational fear reactions where people will avoid common places, situations, or those who suffer from it know there's no threat or danger. This is different than people having everyday fears that make them uneasy; people are generally able to manage those fears and overcome them, allowing them to carry on with their daily activities.

  With Specific Phobias, people understand that their fears make no sense as there is no threat or danger, but feel powerless to stop being afraid. Those with Specific Phobias experience these unreasonable fears in the presence of or in anticipation of a specific object, place, or situation.

  While a specific phobia can arise during childhood, with most people, they emerge during adolescence or early adulthood. The onset is usually sudden and occurs in situations that did not previously cause fear. Specific Phobias are typically focused around animals, insects, germs, heights, thunder, driving, flying, dental or medical procedures, and elevators. They can disrupt daily routines, limit work efficiency, reduce self-esteem, and place strain on relationships. [22]

Anxiety Vs. Depression And Fear

People can face anxiety any day, but an anxiety disorder and everyday anxiety are not necessarily interchangeable. Daily anxiety might include worrying about everyday activities like paying bills or getting a job while an anxiety disorder would be the constant and unsubstantiated worry, which causes significant distress about everyday life.

Daily anxiety would be embarrassment or self-consciousness, while an anxiety disorder would be a person avoiding social situations entirely for fear of being judged or humiliated. Everyday anxiety would include a realistic fear of something while an anxiety disorder is irrational fear and avoidance of an object. And so on.

Often anxiety and depression go hand-in-hand; however, they are not the same thing. Depression is classified by people feeling discouraged, sad, hopeless, unmotivated, or disinterested in life in general for more than two weeks, although like anxiety, the feelings interfere with daily activities. [22]

Depression and anxiety are often grouped, but it is essential to understand that while they have some similarities, they are not the same. "Shared symptoms typically are represented by a negative affect or general distress factor. Symptoms of anhedonia and the absence of positive affect are specific to depression, whereas symptoms of physiological hyperarousal are specific to 'anxiety'," says the American Psychiatric Association (APA). [26]

Worldwide, 322 million people suffer from depression at any given moment, and it occurs most often in women. [26]

With young children especially, depression tends to manifest itself in refusing to go to school, anxiety when separated from parents and worry about parents dying. In teenagers, depression symptoms tend to be irritability, sulkiness, and getting into trouble in school as well as frequent co-morbid anxiety, eating disorders, or substance abuse.

In addition to differences between depression and anxiety, there are also specific characteristics that distinguish between anxiety and fear. Anxiety is "a future-oriented mood state associated with preparation for possible upcoming negative events" while fear is defined as "an alarm response to present or imminent danger (real or perceived)," says the APA. [26]

Additionally, there are three types of physical responses that distinguish anxiety and fear. The verbal-subjective response for anxiety is worry, the overt motor action associated with it is avoidance, and the somato-visceral activity with it is muscle tension. The corresponding responses for fear are thoughts of an imminent threat, escape, and physical symptoms such as sweating, trembling, heart palpitations, and nausea. [26]

However, anxiety and fear do go hand-in-hand, according to the study as more than likely such disorders are "characterized by prototypical fear" which is made up of escape behaviors, physiological arousal, and thoughts of imminent threat. Additionally, the prototypical anxiety that goes along with this fear is comprised of avoidant behaviors, tension, and feelings of future threat. While these symptoms are related to depression, these are also distinct from symptoms of depression. [26]

Children And Anxiety

There is a wide range of anxiety disorders that people around the world face but children, in particular, are usually diagnosed with one or more of a total of 12 different anxiety disorders. These are: [18]

- Separation Anxiety Disorder
- Panic Disorder with or without agoraphobia
- Agoraphobia without a history of panic disorder
- Specific Phobias
- Social Phobia
- Obsessive-Compulsive Disorder
- Posttraumatic Stress Disorder
- Acute Stress Disorder
- Generalized Anxiety Disorder
- Anxiety Disorder due to a medical condition
- Substance-Induced Anxiety Disorder
- An anxiety disorder not otherwise specified

Children do not have to have a single anxiety disorder at a time. About 75 percent of youth are diagnosed with more than one anxiety disorder, and 50 to 60 percent of children diagnosed with an anxiety disorder show evidence of a comorbid affective disorder, which describes two or more conditions appearing within a person. [18]

For some children, fears associated with anxiety tend to intensify and persist. A lot of times, this prevents anxious children from experiencing typical age-related activities that come with childhood. As a result, many anxious adults report that such problems began during their childhood. Overanxious disorders such as separation anxiety and social phobias are present within at least five to 10 percent of children. Therefore, anxiety disorders have a significant impact on children's functioning.

Knowing what anxiety is and its different forms is a critical first step to a parent understanding their child's disorder and how to begin helping them. Use this time to take the crucial first step of engaging with your child by asking how they are feeling. By connecting it to the various symptoms of anxiety that you have learned, it will create a jumping-off point of where to go from here.

As you strive to understand how your child is feeling, not only will you learn more about how to begin helping them, but understanding their mindset will allow you to be able to connect with them on a deeper level. This is something that your child needs right now; someone who understands or at least tries to understand how they feel so they do not feel alone.

What Is Imagination Good For?

Imagination allows us to create, invent, and envision a better future for ourselves. It is what sets humans apart from other animals. To put into action ways to make the world a better place and create the world that we want to live in, we first have to be able to visualize it in our minds or imagination.

The connectivity we experience in the world of the internet was in part started by Steve Jobs. To put into action the creation of this computer that everyone can use and spark the PC movement that led to the internet that we know and love today, we would have had to use imagination.

Jobs began with a thought, a visualization, an image of how he wanted to change the world. With the help of a bit of initiative, motivation, and a team behind him to help, Apple was started in the 1970's. This eventually yielded the universality of computers and soon Apple's staple products, the iPod and the iPhone.

Although Jobs is gone now, because of his imagination right from the beginning that sparked the idea for Apple, the company continues to be an innovator in technology as they consistently put out new versions of iPhones, iPads, computers, and Airpods.

Or how about the worldwide phenomenon, Harry Potter? The internationally best-selling book series begun with a book about a boy with an unusual scar being thrown into the world of wizards and witches.

And how did this incredibly successful franchise begin? With the imagination, of course! Harry Potter could not have started without the initial thought from author JK Rowling. Rowling thought of the idea for Harry Potter and ravenously wrote the first book envisioning in her mind the escapades of Harry Potter and his friends. Soon it became more successful than anyone would have imagined.

What Is Imagination?

Imagination is directly linked to how we perceive the world. The exact definition of imagination is hard to pin down as words such as "image," "imagination" and "imaginative" seem too broad to get to the middle of the power that the world really holds. [20]

Imagination usually tends to fall into three categories: [20]

- As being linked with image, with image is understood as "mental image -a picture in the mind's eye or perhaps a tune running through one's head."
- As being associated with invention and sometimes with originality, insight, felicitous, revealing or striking departure from routine.
- As being linked with false belief, delusion, mistaken memory, or misperception.

Further, philosophers Immanuel Kant and David Hume agree that imagination is a uniting power, which operates in two different dimensions connecting different objects, ideas or images of the same kinds as well as different perceptions of the same object of a given type. [20]

Ultimately, the perception that we have of the world is represented by our imagination. Imagination produces images in the mind which are representatives of our perceptions, Strawson says. It is something that comes from within us, our "internal link."

Another way of thinking about imagination is thinking of things that have not previously existed. To imagine is to think of something, such as the impossible or unfounded, as possible. An imaginative person can think ideas and develop something unique and new. [6]

What is even more profound about someone with a particularly expansive imagination is that they can think of something with "usually some richness of detail." Because of this, imagination is linked to discovery, invention, and originality because it has thought about the possible, rather than the actual. [6]

How Does Imagination Work?

Imagination is suggested to be an involuntary experience, the source of which is an unconscious metaphoric process. This includes memories and thoughts of the self which are "constantly recontextualized, and the link between conscious experience and unconscious memory is provided by metaphor." This is very easy to imagine when it comes to dreams. After all, those are unconscious thoughts that shift without any control on our part.

However, the metaphoric process that we recognize in our dreams is also continuing while we are awake. Therefore, the metaphoric processes that make up imagination are not just a form of thought, but a form of cognition and an interpreter of unconscious memory. [17]

Since the 19th century, chemist Friederich August von Kekule´, noted that the creative imagination could be involuntary and unconscious has articulated it, often. Imagination functions apart from language in its articulation. It is a metaphoric process when operating apart from language, can process fragmented visual, auditory, and other bodily sensations. [17]

There is also a metaphoric transfer of meaning, which can also occur between different sensory modalities, no matter how fragmented the elements are, such as isolated sounds of speech. [17]

How Imagination Contributes To Anxiety And How People Try To Control It

There are times when the imagination can become almost a hindrance to everyday life.

It may be even more common than we realize for our imagination to sneak up on us in our everyday lives and the lives of children as they go to school, interact with friends or meet new people giving them thoughts of the worst-case scenario for a given situation. Those thoughts can very quickly get out of control and lead to more intense worries and anxieties that can prevent them from taking on new situations or even going into familiar positions.

The imagination can introduce fear; fear of the unknown and fear of what could go wrong. Once that fear is launched and starts to take hold of the child, the willpower to carry through with whatever intentions they had can begin to melt away and once it begins to subside can be tough to regain.

However, involuntary imagination is defined one study explored a way that people attempt to control their imagination and the effects that this perceived control has.

This study centers around the idea of counterfactual thinking, which is when life experiences prompt reflection on what could have been done better in the past. For example, the "what could have been thought" that one might have after a car accident would be "At least I put my seatbelt on before I left, I could have been killed." They think of what they did to have control over the situation and focus on that aspect of the event. [8]

Recent research has identified some of the cognitive "rules of mutability." With that, people are more likely to imagine what might have been different about the exceptional aspects of an event, than about the typical aspects, hence trying to regain some control over their imagination as it pertains to such events. With that, the actions people take in a situation are more readily mutated than the actions people do not take. [8]

With this type of thinking, people seek control over their imagination of previous events and focusing on one or another event within a given situation can determine whether a better or worse reality is imagined. Some will yield a more positive way of thinking, and some will produce a more negative way of thinking.

In addition to positive or negative outlooks, the direction of counterfactual thinking will determine an individual's motivation. There are two types of counterfactual thinking which affect people's motivations:[8]

- **Upward Counterfactuals**: This type of thinking would create an improvement in how people see their reality. These counterfactuals prepare us for the future but at the expense of feeling worse in real life.

- **Downward Counterfactuals**: This is considered a worsening of how people see their reality. This type of counterfactual helps us to feel better at the moment, but at the expense of leaving us to feel less prepared for the future.

With counterfactual thinking, people create these counterfactuals about aspects of previous events over which they have perceived control. The alternatives that people imagine shape the experience they have with the event. Overall, controllability influences counterfactuals as people have a general tendency to focus attention on the self. Studies have also suggested that the greater focus on information about the self leads people to take more responsibility for a joint outcome than they should (the self-centered bias). [8]

People crave control over things that happen to them, future and past events, and the way that they recall them. They want to establish control, the study says, or at least an illusion of control. "In turn, the alternatives to the reality that are imagined may shape the affective experience of the event." An individual is more likely to generate counterfactual thinking over either thing they have the most control or at least things that will better serve them in the future.

Imagination is in a lot of ways involuntary and is its own language that people are still trying to understand and, in many cases, find some way to control.

Why Children Need Imagination

When it comes to children and their imagination, imaginative play is an essential step in a child's development. By age three, children are starting to move away from parallel play, which is playing alongside other children with minimal interaction and moving toward more social play with their peers. [14]

One example of this is finding a group of young children in a playgroup playing dress up and assigning roles and costumes. Children at this age fully inhabit imaginary worlds as they learn to adapt to one another's personalities and styles. Fantasy play is an essential step in developing the skills that allow children to separate psychologically from their parents or other caregivers that they depend on and grow into their autonomy and self-esteem.

But the importance of nurturing the imagination does not end at preschool and early grade school years. Often what happens as children get older is that a student's creativity is considered something to be engaged after the hard work is done. It should only be used after class, on the weekend or during a slow day in class with the less disciplined study. However, this view is "wrong and damaging" as imagination should be invoked at any time and in all areas. [6]

When it comes to schools, for example, when teachers are developing lesson plans for their classes, incorporating imaginative aspects into the curriculum is something that is usually glossed over, it's not a routine topic in education programs. It is seen as somehow too vague or not able to be taught. [6]

But everyone is imaginative in some way, shape or form and a child using the imagination in not only the classroom but at home, on the playground or in any other life situation can make them more interested and engaged in the world around them.

How Parents Can Engage Their Child's Imagination

Apart from school, as a parent, you are the first step to nurturing your child's imagination as they grow. Children who utilize their imagination daily are happier, have better social skills, understand emotions, think wisely and become more creative, and parents can be instrumental in ensuring that their child is using their imagination to its fullest.

Fostering your child's imagination starts at home, and there are a few ways that you can encourage this: [2]

- **Read Books**: Reading is a pathway into a new world of adventures for a child and reading to and with your child can help them understand how stories are made, give them the inspiration to create their own as well as establish a life-long love of reading.

- **Tell Stories**: Telling stories from your mind is just as beneficial to children as reading stories because they follow examples of the adults around them, so it inspires them to make up their own stories.

- **Play Games**: This makes for great family-oriented fun that can boost your child's imagination. Some good ones to try are make-believe or charades.

- **Have Real-Life Adventures**: Nothing beats going out and exploring the world with your child. It gives them a chance to get out and see new things to provide them with new ideas to expand their imaginations.

- **Dress Up**: Through dressing up, your child can imagine what it is like to be an entirely different person. Dressing up does not need to be complicated at all, a simple cape or one of your hats or shirts would often suffice. When parents participate in their children's games, the experience becomes even more impactful for them but allows them to lead the imagining as much as possible.

Without imagination, the world would never have experienced "the boy who lived" or any of the other incredibly popular books throughout the years. Without imagination, the world would not have the technological advances that we see today, the iconic TV shows and movies that we all know and love, fantastic art, and architecture that has survived and amazed people for generations, or advances and initiatives that work to make the world a better place. The foundations of all this innovation from creative and imaginative people begin with creative and imaginative children.

Overall, imagination allows us to create the world we want to be a part of, to create what we want to see in the world. It shapes the way we see the world that we live in, which in turn forms the way that we choose to live. After all, imagination is "a necessary ingredient of perception itself." We live in the houses that we live in, drive on the roads that we drive on because they started with someone's imagination and we experience the world the way that we do because we look at the world through the eyes of our imagination.

Correcting Thinking Errors With Smart Talk

The Errors Of Thinking Errors

In the words of Gandhi, "Your beliefs become your thoughts, your thoughts become your words, your words become your actions, your actions become your habits, your habits become your values, your values become your destiny."

With smart talk, that is especially true. The foundation of your words, actions, habits, and values begins with your beliefs and thoughts. But if your thoughts are riddled with negativity or thinking errors, you will no doubt believe that and what follows will not have a positive impact on your life and not assist you in reaching your destiny.

Thinking errors are rampant when it comes to anxiety as they pop up unintentionally and end up being quite convincing because people who experience these thinking errors do not realize that these thoughts do not accurately reflect their situation.

These thinking errors are harmful to children and adults because the people who experience them will respond to their thoughts and belief before they react to the situation itself. They are unconscious until you identify them and flesh them out. Your child does not recognize that a thought may not be accurate and may dramatically overstate adverse outcomes. They then experience consequences such as an accelerated heart rate, butterflies in the stomach, sweaty palms, or feelings of terror. They process information for imagined situations rather than real ones, and they believe their thinking errors. [7]

The Most Common Thinking Errors

- **Catastrophizing**: Assuming the worst-case scenario will occur.
- **Futurizing**: Predicting future negative or fearful situations.

- **Overprobablizing**: Overestimating the probability of negative consequences.

- **Black-And-White Thinking**: Thinking in extremes where everything is all good or all bad.

- **Mind Reading**: Assuming you know what someone else is thinking. [7]

Negative Self-Talk

In addition to thinking errors, negative self-talk also serves to distort a child's thinking. Self-talk, or your inner monologue, can have either a positive or negative influence on a person, but when the self-talk becomes continuously negative, it can reflect a problem. Some examples of negative self-talk are: [16]

- **Globalized Thinking**: This reflects an all-or-nothing attitude and can have negative consequences for how the child feels about themselves in general.

- **Perfectionism**: When one has impossibly high standards for themselves and run themselves down, trying to reach their goals.

- **Obsessing Over Appearances and Negative Actions**: This could be a way of trying to appear "cooler" in front of others or beat others to the punch by making negative statements first.

- **Attention-Seeking**: Verbalizing negative thoughts out loud to get attention from others, especially parents.

- **Lack of Resilience**: Regularly responding to disappointments with negative self-talk leading to avoiding specific experiences or lack of motivation.

- **Internalizing Bullying**: Internalizing words or actions from bullies and turning them into negative self-talk.

Negative self-talk becomes worrisome when the negative self-talk is persistent and pervasive, it is not based in reality, it is impacting the child's relationships or schoolwork, sleeping and eating patterns have changed, or the child makes vague "I don't feel well" statements in the absence of physical symptoms. This could be evidence of low self-esteem, a learning disability, depression, or anxiety.

What Is Smart Talk And How To Use It

Correcting internal thinking errors with smart talk is one of the tools for parents to help their children and reduce the thoughts that lead to anxiety. Using smart talk in trigger situations throughout daily life can diminish reliance on avoidance or safety behaviors. [7]

The key to smart talk is making it a habit. When thinking errors reach the point when they are negatively affecting one's life, they have occurred so often that they have been made into practice. At that point, it is time to change this negative habit into a positive one.

On top of making smart talk into a habit, it can help to consolidate the new learning achieved through exposures, although it should not be used during these exposures. The goal is ultimately to retrain the brain. What usually happens is that people learn how to fear things much more effectively than they learn to extinguish those fears, so retraining requires a lot of practice. [7]

Once a parent has observed and identified the thinking errors that have become a habit for their child, the next step is the four-step process of teaching a child how to use smart talk: [7]

- **Identify Thinking Errors**: The best way to start is by sitting down with your child in a quiet moment and begin by compassionately expressing your worries and explaining in the easiest of terms that you are going to work together, using some "detective work," to figure out what the thinking errors are. For example, if your child is afraid of dogs and can identify that the ultimate reason for being scared of dogs is the fear of being attacked or bitten, the next step is to figure out which of the thinking errors they make that contribute to this fear of dogs. It could be one or more of the five thinking errors listed above. With your child, write down any of the thinking errors you identify.

It is important to note that this is not about pointing out flaws within your child. Instead, the objective should be to remain positive and praise any of the suggestions they make as well as establishing an attitude of curiosity about their thoughts instead of being on a mission to correct them. After all, criticism and pointing out flaws could, in the end, discourage your child and in the end, leave them unwilling to continue with the exercise.

- **Evaluate the Evidence**: An effective strategy for the next step is to begin by asking your child questions about their thoughts so they can consider alternative outcomes. Some of these questions might include: Do these fears (you might want to use a nickname like "Worrybug" to bring the situation down to your child's level) always match what happens in real life? Does what Worrybug tells you always happen, sometimes happen or rarely happen? Was it possible something else happened? Can you think of any times what you thought was going to happen didn't?

Cognitive behavioral therapists call this kind of strategy guided discovery. Like the tradition of Socratic questioning, a teacher, or in this case the parent, ask the student or child a series of questions to stimulate critical thinking to help them reach a conclusion of their own. Instead of an interrogation, guided discovery should feel more like an open-ended, open-minded, collaborative discussion. The steps for guided discovery include asking your child questions, listening to your child's response, summarizing what your child told you, and asking questions that promote alternative ways of thinking about the situation.

- **Generate the Smart Talk**: For step three, it is time to furnish a rational response, otherwise known as the smart talk. Smart talk should correct the thinking errors your child makes in the most straightforward, direct, and simple manner possible. The idea is to keep it short and simple because your child will have to memorize and use it on the go as needed. Another thing to keep in mind is to make sure the smart talk is not merely a pep talk or a reassurance.

Some examples of smart talk phrases you can use and cater to your child's needs are "Just because my friend didn't say hi doesn't mean she doesn't like me," "It's possible but other things are more likely to happen," "Worrybug, you don't really know how it's going to go," or "Nobody is a good mind reader." For some children, especially younger ones, it might be a good idea to use the nickname you have selected in place of fear ("Worrybug" or anything else you might come up with) as part of the smart talk. This will help to not only correct the thinking error but to alert them that they are being triggered. Think of smart talk as editing phrases on a computer where you delete the phrase you wish to change and in its place type in a new one. The same thing applies to replace thinking errors with smart talk.

- **Practice the Smart Talk**: No one ever got better at anything without a little bit of practice. Once you and your child have brainstormed the appropriate smart talk and perfected it, write it down so that you, your child, and other caretakers have a record. Help your child to memorize it so that they can use it exactly as you wrote it together so that they know when to use these notes.

An effective way to practice smart talk is to pretend to be in a trigger situation as children are likely to forget or change their smart talk in the heat of the moment. Imagining being in a trigger situation will arouse their fear, so they will know what it's like to use the smart talk in that situation as well as providing exposure which is the most critical technique in helping your child conquer their fears.

Another way to practice is to make it a game. Have you and your child take turns being the smart talk and the fear and begin a dialogue. The playing the fear will voice your child's thinking error as if they were telling them all the things the thinking error would say to the child in their mind. The one playing smart talk will respond with your child's smart talk phrase.

Things To Remember About Smart Talk

Be aware that, as with any strategy, certain complications or exceptions may occur. Suppose your child does not like smart talk. That's completely okay and not something to trouble you. Some children benefit from smart talk while others do not. If that is the case, your child can still benefit from the process of generating smart talk. [7]

If a child has OCD, smart talk should not be used. The two can have a counter-effect where the child with OCD can turn the smart talk into a ritual, therefore, exacerbating the problem and creating an ineffective treatment. Smart talk should also not be used during exposures because, according to Flynn, it can interfere with inhibitory learning. Instead, take care that smart talk is used either before or after exposures. [7]

Overall, the goal of smart talk is to make it easy for your child to understand and remember, but also make sure that it is useful as far as contradicting the specific thinking errors that your child is experiencing. The key is never to force it on your child or create unrealistic expectations, which can ultimately discourage your child. Keep it relaxed and keep it fun. [7]

Taking Charge Of The Imagination

Smart talk is an excellent way for children to relieve thinking errors which create anxiety. With children and anyone for that matter, sometimes a person's inner dialogue can be their worst enemy as it perpetuates thoughts of failure, disaster, untrue assumptions about how others perceive you, and more. These debilitating thoughts, directed at oneself or the situation a person finds themselves in, can be enough to cripple their willpower and emotional stability.

But it is not just words or thinking errors that can tie your child down and prevent them from experiencing life to its fullest extent. Your child's imagination can create images that are just as scary, if not scarier, than thinking errors.

One definition of imagination sums up perfectly the way that imagination can play a role in creating anxiety for your child: Imagination creates a mental image or "a picture in the mind's eye or perhaps a tune running through one's head." It can be associated with an invention that can be an immense departure from reality, and it can be linked with false belief, delusion, mistaken memory, or misperception. [20]

All of this mixed with the incredibly inventive and impressionable mind of a child is the perfect recipe for the imagination to scare and create anxieties for a child. [20]

As we established previously, imagination is in many ways, involuntary. Sometimes it is not possible to prevent images from appearing in your mind as they occur in a spur of the moment. However, it is possible to control the way we react to our imagination. In children, establishing these coping strategies in a fun and easy way, either through words, implementing worry buddies to assist in such situations or drawing the scary thing and changing it, can be critical when addressing such issues.

Worry Words

One of the most basic ways to tackle an onset of anxiety is with words. Using words to combat your child's anxiety can serve to empower them and allow them to feel secure in moments of fear.

The best thing to do is to create a list of worry words to use against anxiety together. Sit down with your child and write out a few ideas. Some examples of these can be "I am not afraid" "I am good enough" and "I will not let fear win." It is best to keep the worry words simple so that your child can remember them during anxious moments. Practice them with your child and go over situations where they might be useful. Then when your child is finally face-to-face with a situation that triggers their anxiety, they already have some tools to stop the anxiety.

Worry Buddies

One thing that may help a child cope with anxiety is a comfort object or a worry buddy. Children with anxiety or traumas often turn to a companion, whether it be a blanket, a stuffed animal, or a doll. It allows them to express what they are feeling in a way that they may not feel comfortable doing to anyone else as well as deal with complicated feelings. [9]

There are typically three reasons why a child might opt to use a comfort object: either it represents a phase in their development, a defense mechanism against separation anxiety or as a neutral sphere where their experiences and feelings are not challenged as they would be otherwise. What often occurs is that these objects can be incorporated into the child's work and play; your child may use the object while reading a book, doing homework or going down a slide at the park. [9]

Also called a transitional object, in addition to providing comfort in troublesome times, they provide an understanding of human development as the way the child interacts with the object becomes indicative of how they will interact with others later in life and maintain social relationships. It is representative of the child's developmental milestones and for the child represents a stable and predictable world.

For the time being, it invites emotional well-being for the child, and without the object, true feelings might be suppressed, concealed or dismissed as the child has no other way to cope with or contend with the world around them. [9]

Draw It And Change It

Another strategy that can be especially useful when it comes to imagination is drawing the thing the child is afraid of and changing it into something that is not as scary.

Art therapy is widely used to treat anxiety. Diane

Waller, professor of art psychotherapy, wrote about the process and outcomes of art therapy on children. There she says that "the aim of art therapy is to facilitate positive change through engagement with the therapist and the art materials in a safe environment." Although technically art therapy typically involves the use of a therapist assisting the child, the effects that art and drawing have on kids are plentiful as Waller describes in her report. [24]

Waller lists several fundamental principles of art therapy. One is that visual image-making is an essential aspect of the human learning process. Children are still learning about themselves and how to deal with their emotions, and while anxiety can perpetuate the images that they see, visual image-making can help them work through these fears as a natural aspect of human nature.

Another fundamental is that "art can act as a 'container' for powerful emotions. These can be emotions such as fear and worry that are making a child feel anxious. Allowing a child to draw out what they are feeling can act as a form of self-expression for their emotions." [24]

Art can also be a means of communication between the child and the therapist. This is great if you are taking your child to a therapist, but even if you are practicing drawing in the comfort of your own home, this fundamental still applies. Instead of a therapist, seeing what your child is drawing and having discussions about it can open the door for communication between you and your child that may not have been possible in the past. [24]

Working with your child on drawing out their fears and then changing it into something that is not as scary can open the door to exploring their feelings and different coping mechanism that you and your child may not have considered before. It can be an easy way to make the fears that your child may be having into a game and turn it into something less intimidating.

Change begins to take place as a result of the child learning that it is possible to have feelings, whether it is fear, sadness, worry or more, as well as to express their feelings safely through the art, and in the knowledge that the therapist, or you as a parent, will not retaliate. [24]

How the action of drawing their feelings takes form is entirely dependent on the child. Sometimes it is enough for them to make the art and exchange only a few words with you or an art therapist. At other times the child may speak about it, or be prompted to tell a story about it. Being able to externalize and share distressed feelings with an empathetic adult has proved very helpful to generations of unhappy and disturbed children, "although expression of feelings alone is usually not enough to bring about significant changes. It is a beginning." Expressing feelings at one given moment is not going to result in a cure, but it is a beginning for opening up further dialogue and exploration into additional methods.

Overall, art made in a safe space may enable a child to explore and express feelings that they cannot easily put into words. [24]

Manipulating Thoughts To Become More Realistic And Reduce Anxiety

Cognitive Therapy Skills

Negative thoughts are never conducive to a happy and productive lifestyle, and this is very true for children. If your child falls into the category of one or more anxiety disorder and negative thoughts are ruling their life, it helps to find ways to turn these negative thoughts into more realistic thoughts. One of the ways to do this is by enhancing their cognitive therapy skills.

Cognitive therapy skills involve responding to and modifying thoughts to help one cope better in their daily lives and to feel less anxious. [3]

The main goal of utilizing cognitive therapy skills is to gather evidence that relates to the feelings and anxious thoughts that one may be having. By enhancing their cognitive therapy skills, your child can make informed choices about issues that affect them. Gathering these facts about their feelings allows them to evaluate them and work through them in a calm and focused manner and in turn they can do something with them and problem solve.

With that, it also gives them a window to understanding that there might not be anything they can do about the situation they are in, and that is okay. Working through their anxious thoughts in this way will allow your child to not only reduce their anxiety by taking control of all situations but realize that not every situation is going to be in their favor and therefore they can accept this fact and let go of efforts to control and kind of go with the flow. [3]

Negative Automatic Thoughts And Cognitive Distortions

Anxious thoughts can have a snowball effect. The resulting negative thoughts, avoidant behaviors, and anxiety symptoms serve to fuel your child's anxiety and ultimately make it worse as they pile on top of each other.

One thing that your child may be experiencing is negative automatic thoughts. These are negative thoughts that come to us automatically whenever we are feeling anxious, depressed, angry, or frustrated. It is not necessarily something you can stop, as you don't see or feel it coming. But in the moment, in the heat of emotion, the negative automatic thoughts come and only make the feeling of anxiety, frustration, etc., worse: [3]

- **Overestimating the Likelihood of Negative Events Happening**: This is one of the most common occurrences when experiencing anxiety. We often imagine something negative will happen even if we know that it is unlikely.

- **Catastrophizing**: When your child is catastrophizing, they may feel like they are unable to cope and find ways to avoid the catastrophe they are imagining.

- **Beliefs That Anxiety Itself Is Dangerous**: Often, it is possible to have negative thoughts about anxiety itself and think it is possible to lose control or not be able to function.

- **Belief That One Cannot Tolerate Discomfort, Pain or Negative Events**: Much like having believing anxiety is dangerous your child may feel as though they cannot function through discomfort, pain or negative events and worry about what would happen to them if something like this happened.

- **Negative Thoughts About Ourselves, Others, And the World**: Your child may make negative assumptions about themselves or make blanket statements such as "I can't do this." These can make them feel more anxious.

Another thing your child could be experiencing is cognitive distortions. Unlike negative automatic thoughts, these are patterns of thinking influenced by emotions. Cognitive distortions are often extreme, very general, and emphasize negatives at the expense of positives. Some examples of these are: [3]

- **Black-And-White Thinking**: This involves thinking in extremes with no middle ground.
- **Catastrophizing**: With catastrophizing, your child will predict the worst-case scenario and react to disappointment and failure as if it is the end of the world.
- **Jumping to Conclusions**: This involves assuming the worst without checking the evidence. Most times, the worst will not happen, but when jumping to conclusions, your child will not realize this.

- **Ignoring the Positive**: Focusing entirely on negative thoughts and ideas, they also reject the positives as if it cannot happen.

- **Magnifying and Minimizing**: This involves making shortcomings seem more prominent and more important than they are while making positives aspects of the self seem unimportant or nonexistent.

- **Labels**: Like the negative automatic thought of thinking negative thoughts about oneself and the world, labels involve making blanket statements about oneself or others.

- **Reasoning from Our Emotions**: Your child may feel that just because they feel a certain way that indicates the truth about a situation. If they feel depressed or fearful, then they may feel that the situation they are in seems just as hopeless.

Using Cognitive Therapy Skills

It is essential to emphasize the benefits of not only introducing cognitive therapy skills to your child but practicing them as well. Modifying thoughts make your brain change, and consistent practice keeps the brain functioning well. It goes back to the importance of making the behavior a habit.

Cognitive therapy skills can be used to relieve most types of anxiety, especially in cases where you can identify negative thoughts that make you feel worse in certain situations as well as in anxiety triggered by worries about the future or negatives thoughts about the self. [3]

Cognitive therapy skills revolve around asking yourself questions about what you may be feeling. The answers that you come up with to these questions are considered a rational response and allow you to take an objective look at why you are feeling this way. Two of the basic restructuring questions you can start with are how likely is it that this event will happen, and if it did happen, how bad would it be. [3]

To further help your child work on skills to transform their thoughts into more realistic ones and further enhance cognitive therapy skills, it might be useful to give cognitive behavioral therapy a try. Cognitive behavioral therapy is an effective treatment for children and adolescents with anxiety.

Cognitive behavioral therapy emerged from two areas of experimental psychology: learning theory and cognitive psychology. But it was not widely accepted as a form of treatment until around the 1960's and 1970's. Up to this point, over 40 studies have been conducted to examine the effectiveness of cognitive behavioral therapy in youth. Randomized clinical trials indicate that cognitive behavioral therapy is extremely effective in treating children as approximately two-thirds of the children treated with cognitive behavioral therapy will be free of their primary diagnosis at post-treatment. Usually, cognitive behavioral therapy sessions take about 12 to 16 weeks, and they rarely will last beyond six months. [3]

The primary goal of this treatment is to change maladaptive learning and thought patterns. What is vital about cognitive behavioral therapy for children is that it is distinct from other psychosocial interventions. For starters, cognitive behavioral therapy for children attempts to understand the root of the problem on to the degree that it gives way to be able to intervene in the here and now. With that, it is more critical to the treatment to work towards a cure for the child as soon as possible. Additionally, the treatment is focused on addressing the factors that maintain the symptoms of anxiety disorders more so than what gave rise to those disorders. [3]

It also takes a skills-building approach. Cognitive behavioral therapy sessions for children are only an initial step in the learning process but, again, practice is essential in retaining the cognitive therapy skills that will ultimately reduce your child's anxiety. These sessions will introduce the skills as well as methods for practice as well as methods for problem-solving in the moment of anxiety.

But cognitive behavioral therapy does not just involve treatment on the part of the child to transform your child's way of thinking. It is just as vital that you, as a parent, are involved as well. Cognitive behavioral therapy introduces new skills for the parents to take on and incorporate into the family to further assist the child with reducing their anxiety. Sometimes it can even involve the child's teachers, siblings, and peers as well.

Studies have shown that family involvement in cognitive behavioral therapy is extremely beneficial to the child. There is a high rate, over 70 percent, of children who respond well to cognitive behavioral therapy with parental involvement. It is also useful when it includes family interventions. [25]

When it comes to parental involvement with cognitive behavioral therapy, there are a few things that parents should try to implement in their day-to-day interactions with their child. This will maintain the cognitive behavioral therapy skills the child has learned: [25]

- Give choices when your child is indecisive and encourage them to make their own choices. Do not make choices for them.
- Allow your child to struggle and learn to fix it on their own by trial and error rather than making choices for them.
- Label and accept your child's emotional responses, but do not criticize them as this could discourage your child.
- Encourage your child to acquire new self-help skills to help relieve their anxiety.

Parents are significant agents of change, and they must work together with the child to practice cognitive therapy skills. This may involve changing your parental behaviors and approaches to your child's anxiety. Parents, of course, play a major role in the lives of their children, and when working with your child to transform their thoughts, you act as a coach for the child in everyday situations. It takes commitment on the part of the child and the parent to work. [25]

Turning Anxious Thoughts Into Useful Thoughts

Anxious Thoughts

When using cognitive therapy skills, your child will ultimately focus on turning their anxious thoughts into ones that are more realistic to what they are experiencing or will experience in real life instead of the negative outcomes they envision through their cognitive distortions and negative automatic thoughts.

However, that does not necessarily mean those new thoughts are positive or will help them to see themselves in a more positive light. Help your child take it a step further by turning their negative and anxious thoughts into positive, healthy thinking.

In addition to having negative automatic thoughts and cognitive distortions contribute to their anxiety, those who experience anxiety are more likely to have irrational beliefs about themselves and fear negative perceptions of themselves by others. [4]

People with anxiety articulate less rational thoughts when confronted with stressful social-evaluative situations than people who are less involved with criticism of themselves. It does not matter what your child's personality is. Whether introverted or extroverted, when it comes to an anxiety disorder, negative thoughts about themselves are more likely to translate to your child fearing that others have the same views about them. [4]

Your child could have a negative automatic thought that makes them worried about how their classmates perceive them. If they have social anxiety, for example, this negative automatic thought may be even more persistent in their everyday lives leading them to assume that their peers don't like them, that they think they are weird or less intelligent or that something is wrong with them. This is more than likely not the case, but having an anxiety disorder makes it seem all the more real that their classmates have a negative view of them leading your child to have a negative view of themselves. [4]

Strategies For Creating Positive Thoughts

Healthy thinking helps prevent and control anxiety. Negative thoughts and cognitive distortions lead to increased worry and fear, which leads to the ongoing cycle of anxiety within your child. As we discussed in the last chapter, cognitive behavioral therapy ultimately strives to replace negative thoughts with more encouraging ones, and changing your child's thinking takes time. So, practicing healthy thinking every day will eventually become second nature.

There are a few strategies you can help your child with to help them get better at using healthy thinking: [12]

- **Notice and Stop Thoughts**: The best way to do this is to stop using negative self-talk. And that's hard because it becomes so ingrained in the mind without even realizing it but before you know it you're putting yourself down always which has an impact on the mind. Self-talk does not always have to be negative and not useful to a positive mindset. It is what you make of it, and on the more positive side, it can be rational and hopeful. Walk your child through the steps of improving self-talk as previously discussed to help them have a more positive inner dialogue.

- **Ask About Thoughts**: When your child experiences negative thoughts, instruct them to ask themselves whether the thoughts they are having are helpful or unhelpful. For example, if your child is continuously catastrophizing, saying that they will never be able to get through their math class, have them stop and look at what they are saying to themselves. Does the evidence in front of them support their thoughts? Maybe they are doing well with the homework or the tests, or their teacher is very willing to help them improve their math skills. There can also be more that they can do to improve, maybe they need to take more time to practice or pay more attention. What can they do, or what are they already doing, that suggests evidence contrary to the negative thoughts they are having?

- **Journaling**: This could be useful to give your child a visual way to examine and engage with the negative thoughts that make them anxious. It will help them to see what unhelpful thoughts they are having and replace them with helpful ones. Have your child write down the negative thoughts that they have either throughout the day or at the end of the day. Next, to it, have them write down a helpful message to correct the thought. Their negative thought might be, "I'll never feel normal. I worry about everything all the time." The correcting helpful thought that they write next to it can be something like "I've laughed and relaxed before. I can practice letting go of my worries.

By putting these steps into practice, positive thoughts will soon come to your child naturally. By stopping, asking, and choosing their thoughts along with journaling their thoughts, it will make them better aware of their self-talk and lead them to work towards creating a happier, more positive mindset.

The Importance Of Having Coping Skills For Different Times, Places And Stressors

Coping skills are specific efforts, behavioral and psychological, that people employ to tolerate, master, reduce, or minimize stressful life events. Because anxiety disorders are the most common type of disorder diagnosed in children, efficient early prevention, and intervention is essential. Part of that includes teaching a child coping skills. [21]

Cognitive coping is a cognitive way of managing the intake of emotionally stressful life events. The different types of cognitive coping are distinguished by a predominant focus on decreasing negative affect in response to stressful situations. They serve as a mediator and moderator of the association between stress and psychological well-being. [15]

This study says that the coping strategies of children with anxiety disorders and children without anxiety disorders are greatly distinguished. Therefore, cognitive coping is especially crucial to children who suffer from anxiety disorders as they experience significantly more stressful situations than their non-anxiety disordered counterparts. They also perceive situations as more threatening.

Children who do not suffer from anxiety disorders tend to use adaptive cognitive coping strategies when it comes to stressful situations and life events. These types of coping strategies include positive refocusing and positive reapproval. However, children who do have anxiety disorders will tend to use more maladaptive cognitive coping strategies, which include rumination, self-blame, and catastrophizing in response to negative situations which only serve to reinforce symptoms of anxiety. [15]

These thought patterns apply to a range of anxiety disorders, including social anxiety, generalized anxiety disorder, and separation anxiety, to name a few. Additionally, children with anxiety disorders tend to think more about the feelings associated with negative life experiences as well as focus more on the negative aspects of the events and situations they experience. Because of this, they employ more maladaptive coping strategies. Unfortunately, the negative consequence of this can be that they will struggle to cope with adverse life events in adulthood if more positive coping strategies are not learned. This is why it is of the utmost importance to intervene as soon as possible. [15]

Childhood is a sensitive period in life. Children are becoming progressively more aware of their internal experiences, experiencing a gradual maturation of cognitive capacities, developing more sophisticated cognitive strategies to regulate the emotions they are still discovering and are becoming more able to control their emotions in response to stress in a cognitive way. Because of this, it is important to make sure early on that your child is enacting positive coping strategies and knows when to use these strategies.

Coping strategies typically fall into two categories: problem-solving strategies and emotion-focused strategies. [21]

Problem-solving strategies revolve around those efforts to alleviate stressful situations. These are usually focused on problems that a person can potentially control; in the case of your child, this may be school-related problems or family or friends-related problems. Emotion-focused coping strategies focus on efforts to regulate the emotional consequences of stressful or potentially stressful events in life. These are useful more for situations that are beyond one's control, like specific health problems.

The type of coping strategy that will be used depends not only on the situation and whether it is controllable or not, but it also depends on personal style as some people cope more actively than others. [21]

Coping strategies also fall into two different ways of coping: active coping and avoidant coping. With active coping strategies, these are behavioral or psychological responses that are designed to change the nature of the stressor or how one thinks about it. Whereas, avoidant coping strategies lead people into activities or mental states that keep them from directly addressing and dealing with stressful events.

Avoidant coping strategies are usually a marker for adverse response to stressful events, so the ultimate goal is to get to the point where one can cope as it leads to better ways of coping with stressful events. [21]

Types Of Coping Skills

Calming Skills

Calming skills are a type of coping skill that is often used as a supplement to cognitive behavioral therapy skills such as exposure therapy and cognitive thinking skills. [19]

Often when a child is experiencing anxiety, they may experience symptoms such as muscle tension, restlessness, headaches, clenched jaw, and difficulty concentrating. Calming skills address these symptoms directly by addressing anxiety from the standpoint of the body. They do this by reducing muscle tension, slowing down the breathing, and calming the mind. [19]

The main goal of calming skills is to learn how to breathe in a way that promotes a calm mindset as well as relaxation. Additionally, with calming skills, your child will learn to slow down their mental activity, increase body awareness, and decrease body tension to combat typical symptoms that come with anxiety. [19]

With practice, your child will ultimately learn how and when to use these skills.

However, calming skills should not be a replacement for exposure and cognitive therapy skills. Ensure that your child knows the importance of practicing them daily as they help to promote relaxation within the body for times where anxiety is present. Calming skills should be used during times of stress to prevent avoidance actions during anxiety episodes, but they should not be used in times of panic to get rid of anxiety. Think of them as a companion to exposure and cognitive therapy skills.

Some examples of calming skills are:[19]

- **Breathing**: One of the symptoms of anxiety episodes is uneven breathing. By regulating your child's breathing, they will be able to begin to calm the anxious feelings within their bodies. The process of slowing their breathing to communicate safety to the mind is called slow diaphragmatic breathing. One of the ways they can do this is to sit comfortably in a quiet environment, place their hand on their stomach or chest, breathe in and out slowly, and to count to five or ten.

- **Mindful Walk**: When your child feels anxious, sometimes it may help to release some of the bodily tension by taking a walk. This can entail you walking with them around the neighborhood, through the park or taking a walk around the house. They can incorporate breathing techniques into the walk and encourage them to focus on what is around them and how their body feels as they walk.

- **Grounding**: These are strategies that distract from emotional pain and allow your child to focus on the present. This can be done at any time using the mind or the senses. Some techniques that grounding involves include listing the sounds around you, counting the objects you see, count to 10 or say the alphabet, touch various objects around you or grabbing onto a chair as hard as you can.

- **Progressive Muscle Relaxation**: PMR promotes the absence of tension within the body. The aim is to learn to gradually release tension through daily exercises of tensing and releasing muscles. It communicates calmness and safety throughout the body, reducing the need to activate a fight or flight response. These do not need to be complicated; your child doesn't need to develop a vigorous workout routine where they go to the gym every day. One of the ways your child can practice PMR is by flexing their bicep, holding the tension for about five seconds and then releasing.

- **Positive Self Talk**: This technique returns to the act of reducing the negative automatic thoughts your child experiences. One way your child can practice positive self-talk is by making a list of their best qualities and attributes and repeating these statements throughout the day. Practicing a combination of positive self-talk strategies will serve to create a sense of calmness and positivity within your child.

- **Mindfulness**: These techniques originated in Buddhist meditation techniques but in recent years have been well studied and well utilized to promote relaxation. The goal is to describe all experiences non-judgmentally and objectively focusing on facts about the present moment, much like cognitive therapy skills. To practice mindfulness, have your child sit quietly in a relaxing space while practicing slow diaphragmatic breathing. Instruct them to notice that their mind will wander to different thoughts and assure them that this is okay. Have them observe, either out loud or internally, how the mind wanders and slowly begin to pull it back into their breathing.

- **Applied Relaxation**: This technique aims to increase the ability to relax quickly. It involves a set of calming skills enacted in stages over time:
  - **Progressive Muscle Relaxation**: Practice two to three times a day for two weeks.
  - **Release-Only Relaxation**: This is like progressive muscle relaxation, but instead of tensing the muscles first, focus on releasing tension. After practicing progressive muscle relaxation, do this in seven to eight-minute increments each day.
  - **Cue Controlled Relaxation**: Release all the tension throughout the body as if on cue to fully relax. This is done in two to three minutes.
  - **Differential Relaxation**: In this stage, your child will practice relaxing during daily activities to incorporate relaxation into their daily lives. This should be practiced in non-stressful situations.

- **Rapid Relaxation**: With practice, your child will be able to relax quickly in a variety of situations within 20 to 30 seconds.

- **Applied Relaxation**: At the final stage, your child will be able to incorporate these techniques into anxiety-inducing situations.

It takes time to master, but with practice, applied relaxation could be a great coping skill.

- **Listening to Music**: Music, especially classical music, ambient music, repetitive music and sounds of nature, have been widely proven to create a calming mindset. To ensure that your child gets daily or weekly benefits from listening to relaxing music, play it in the car, while doing homework or before bedtime.

- **Smells**: Aromatherapy has also been widely used for centuries to encourage relaxation through scent. To have your child receive the benefits from aromatherapy, you may want to light scented candles or incense around the house. Relaxing scents include lavender and rose.

- **Nature**: Experiencing nature is a natural form of relaxation. Seeing things like beaches or falling leaves or flowers may help your child relax. As often as possible, take your child to the park, the beach, or for a walk through the woods for an opportunity to get out and experience the relaxing aspects of nature. It will also provide an excellent chance for them to play.

- **Hot Baths**: Sometimes a relaxing hot bath after a long day helps to calm a person down tremendously. Bubble baths may be especially fun for a child and allow an opportunity to take their mind off whatever may be triggering their anxiety. It may also be an opportunity to use a scented bubble bath to incorporate aromatherapy.

- **Meditation**: Meditation goes hand-in-hand with mindfulness as it originated with Buddhist and

Hindu traditions and is widely used today as a technique to relax and reduce anxiety. Mindfulness is one type of meditation. However, several kinds of meditation can promote calmness and happiness within your child. For example, with breath awareness meditation, you should have your child sit quietly in a seated position and take slow breaths. They should focus solely on their breathing during this process and ignore all other thoughts. This will help clear their minds as they focus on this one thing.

- **Autogenics**: This is a relaxation technique developed to reduce anxiety and can be incorporated into cognitive behavioral therapy. To practice autogenics, have your child find a quiet space, lie on the floor, and take slow breaths. Then they will repeat statements such as "I am completely calm," "My heartbeat is calm" and "My arms are warm," working their way down their entire body focusing on relaxing each body part.

- **Body Scan**: Anxiety often causes symptoms such as bodily tension or shaking. During body scans, your child focuses on calming their entire body. Have them start at the top of their head and work their way down to their feet, focusing on calming each part of their body and release any tension held there. One way to think of it is to tell your child to imagine a wave washing over them, and each part of their body lets go of tension as the wave washes over them.

- **Balloon Breathing**: To control your child's breathing, have them visualize blowing up a balloon. Blowing too hard or too fast will cause the balloon to pop so they must inhale and exhale slowly to blow up the balloon. After a few slow breaths, have them think of one word they would write on the balloon that contributes to their anxiety and imagine releasing it off into the sky.

Distraction Skills

Distraction skills are another type of coping skill. These are taught during cognitive behavioral therapy and serve to distract and draw attention away from intrusive thoughts.

Three principal approaches come with distraction skills. One of them involves cognitive approaches. These include activities such as reading aloud or humming. Behavioral distractions include interpersonal activities such as interacting with others. Finally, physiological distractions involve actions through the body or the senses. These include many types of calming techniques, exercise and listening to music. [5]

It is important to note that, like calming skills, distraction skills are also meant to be used in conjunction with cognitive therapy skills and exposure therapy. [5]

Some example of distraction skills are: [5]

- **Write A Story**: One of the best ways to take your child's mind off whatever is making them anxious is by allowing them to focus their mind on something else and be creative. Writing a story can consume your child for either a few minutes, or for hours, but it will undoubtedly allow them to think of something else and allow them to create instead of focusing on the thing that is triggering their anxiety.

- **Read**: Reading is the ultimate way to immerse yourself in a different world and become invested in someone else's life and adventures for a while. Indeed, it is more challenging to get some children to read than others, but it is a matter of finding something that will keep them continuously engaged whether that is a picture book, a novel or a comic book. But once your child is immersed in the world of a book, they will have something to distract them from their anxiety.

- **Playing**: The natural instinct of a child is to play. This is how they explore the world and their imagination in these formative years. When experiencing worries that come from anxiety, this can easily override the desire to play. Encourage your child to play with their toys or play pretend. Even better would be to play with your child yourself. Pull out a board game, a card game or a video game to help them focus on something besides what is worrying them.

- **Exercise**: Exercise is not only a great distraction to anxiety, but it also releases endorphins and adrenaline that promote happiness and relaxation throughout the body. One way you can encourage a lifestyle within your child that includes continuous exercise is signing them up for a class such as dance or gymnastics or a sports team. Getting your child the right amount of exercise does not have to involve signing them up for classes as transportation and money can be an issue. Do simple exercises like jumping jacks and running while at home or go for walks.

- **Listening To Music**: Listening to music is a calming skill, but it can also be considered a distraction skill as well because it involves engaging the senses. You can have them listen to either calming music or their favorite songs to distract from their anxieties.

- **Singing**: A natural antidepressant, singing releases endorphins that cause happiness and oxytocin, which overall reduces stress anxiety. If your child naturally enjoys singing, this may be a no brainer. If your child isn't usually the type to sing very often, it may be useful to try singing with them showing them that it can be fun.

- **New Toys**: While this distraction skill doesn't recommend spoiling your child, new toy every once in a while can serve to distract your child from whatever anxious thought they may be having at least for the moment. It appeals to the desire of a child to play and imagine and encourages them to be a kid instead of worrying about the world around them.

- **Fun Activities**: Fun activities serve as another way to give your child something to do that will take their mind off their anxious thoughts. These can include various outdoor activities or taking day trips to museums or amusement parks.

- **Drawing**: Another way to engage your child's imagination, like Waller said, drawing serves as a container for a child's emotions. Encouraging your child to draw can serve as a way for them to directly address the thoughts and fears they may be having, or to draw whatever makes then happy.

- **Watch A Movie**: Much like reading, watching a video allows your child to immerse their thoughts in the lives and adventures of someone else. With the visuals that a movie brings, this can be especially useful for distracting your child, especially when it comes to action and comedy movies.

- **Count Backward from A Large Number**: A simple technique, but an effective one. These can be used at any time, even in the moment of anxious situations. Instruct your child to take a moment to pause and begin to count backward from 50, 100, or whatever number seems suitable in the moment as needed.

- **Focus on Your Surroundings**: Very rarely do we take a moment to stop and observe the world around us. If your child can take the time to stop and take a look at what's around them, it may very much help to distract from what is making them anxious. It would be even more useful not just to name the objects that they see and maybe describe their features.

- **Help with Household Chores**: Although this may at first seem mundane to your child, helping them to become engaged in the task at hand allows them to put their mind on something. It is even more useful not just to tell them to do chores like wash dishes or clean their room, make it into a game so they will have a reason to have fun and feel relaxed. For example, set a 30 or 60 second time limit on cleaning their room. They will race around the room so focused on completing the task at hand that their worries of the moment will be forgotten.

- **Spend Time with Family Members**: A little bit of social interaction could be just what your child needs to distract from their anxiety. Interacting with family members, grandparents, cousins, aunts, and uncles are beneficial because they are familiar and could serve to make your child feel more comfortable than they would around their peers.

- **Computer Games**: Technology is everywhere these days, and it indeed serves as a distraction for most people. With endless apps and games, a phone or a computer can keep your child distracted for hours, but the American Heart Association recommends that children spend a maximum of two hours in front of a screen per day.

Physical Skills

Physical Skills are used by 14 percent of people to cope with stress and anxiety, and for a good reason. It may be one of the number one techniques recommended by health care professionals to begin to reduce stress and anxiety. [22]

It comes with many physical benefits that have long been established as well as mental benefits as it enhances overall cognitive function, which can be especially helpful when stress has depleted energy or the ability to concentrate. Mostly when stress affects the brain, the body feels the impacts as well through its many nerve connections to the brain.

However, many forms of physical activity release endorphins, chemicals in the brain that act as natural painkillers, which reduce stress. Overall, the more physical activity your child partakes in, especially at times when anxiety is likely to be triggered, it can act as an excellent coping mechanism. [22]

Some examples of physical coping skills are:

- **Dance**: A fantastic way to get exercise without feeling very much like you are exercising. Not only does dancing provide a good workout and a way to have fun, when practicing choreography, but it also utilizes the mind and the body, and in combination with music, it provides immense stress relief. If this is something that your child enjoys, it might even be beneficial to enroll them in a dance class.

- **Exercise**: The physical benefits of exercise seem endless. In addition to helping a person stay physically fit and fight diseases, it has also been shown to improve mental fitness as well. Regular aerobic exercise has been found to decrease tension in the body, elevate the mood, improve sleep, and improve self-esteem. For your child, exercise does not need to be complicated. You can do simple exercises with them like jumping jacks or lunges or enroll them in a sport or class. On average, kids need an hour of physical activity per day.

- **Walk**: This is as effective as vigorous exercise when it comes to anxiety, especially when it includes a quiet walk through nature or some other beautiful scenery. Walking also releases endorphins that help with improving the mood and reducing stress.

- **Bike Riding**: Another way for your child to get active, riding a bike seems to be an essential part of childhood. Whether it's riding through the neighborhood or the park, bike riding can provide a way for your child to be active and distract from anxious thoughts, especially when done with a friend or you as a parent.

- **Sports**: Playing sports is known to reduce anxiety levels, raise energy, and improve mood. The team aspect of sports is also important as interacting with others is another way to cope with anxiety.

- **Get Enough Sleep**: Sleep is essential for physical and mental functionality. Getting enough sleep affects the brain, which directly affects mental health so getting enough sleep during the week is like hitting a reset button in your mind allowing it enough time to repair itself after a long day. Generally, children ages four through 12 should get at least 10 hours of sleep per night.

- **Running**: Running is another form of physical activity that helps people relax by releasing endorphins that also improve their mood and improve self-confidence. For your child, this could mean running around the yard, the park, taking a run through the neighborhood or running at school during recess. If you, a friend, or a sibling run with your kid in a race or game like Red Light Green Light that's even better.

- **Jumping Rope**: Another form of physical activity that helps to increase serotonin and reduce stress, jumping rope is an activity that your child can do alone or with you, friends, or siblings.

- **Slow Down**: Although increased physical activity is good for reducing anxiety, so is an occasional decrease in physical activity. In the world we live in today everything seems to move so fast, and everyone wants to get things done as soon as possible. Encourage your child to slow down and takes things easy sometimes, especially during anxious moments.

- **Eat Well**: Just like getting enough sleep and exercise, the body cannot function properly without a well-balanced diet. Ensure that your child is eating from a range of food groups, eating a healthy breakfast every day and limits junk food.

- **Take Breaks**: Another way to slow down the pace of life, sometimes it's just a good idea to take a break from everything. Especially during moments of anxiety, encourage your child to step back and take a break to do something pleasurable to take their mind off their anxiety.

- **Get A Good Routine**: Sometimes stress and anxiety can emerge when daily activities are unpredictable. Assist your child by establishing a daily routine that includes set tiles for meals, bedtime, and other significant aspects of the day. This can help regulate the day so that your child knows what is coming next and does not have to worry about the future in that respect.

- **Eat A Little Chocolate**: Chocolate, especially dark chocolate without a lot of sugar and added ingredients, is great for reducing anxiety and stress because it contains compounds that improve a person's mood and it reduces cortisol, the stress hormone that helps to cause anxiety.

- **Laugh**: A good laugh now and then can improve mental health and create an overall positive outlook on life. It increases oxygen within the body and also releases stress-reducing hormones as exercise does. It acts as a natural muscle relaxer which can reduce stress overall.

- **Catharsis**: This is the process of releasing strong, pent up emotions. These acts can include yelling, punching a pillow, or squeezing something. While not something to do all the time, letting off a bit of tension now and then could be a good idea.

Processing Skills

Processing Skills come in handy during that moment that often happens during a moment of anxiety where people freeze for a moment. During that moment, everything seems to go blank; your child cannot process what is going on as the anxiety has overtaken them, and their body is trying to compose itself. They are not processing information as fast as they would be otherwise, and it takes longer to respond, make decisions, and size up situations. [23]

Slow processing or worries about slow processing can create anxiety. Your child can worry about trailing behind others as they know the experience of going blank and processing not working at a normal pace at that moment can give them anxiety before going into certain situations such as tests.

It can also be possible that your child has slow processing in one area, such as math. This can make going to math class an anxious experience for them. They are afraid to be called on in class or asked to write on the board for fear that they will not be able to process the subject as well as other students, and their worries can give them an even slower processing speed. [23]

Processing coping skills can give your child a chance to stop and recollect their thoughts in moments of anxiety. Some examples of processing skills are: [13]

- **Feelings as Colors**: Also called rainbow breathing, to do this have your child sit or lie down in a comfortable position and have them inhale, hold for a few seconds and exhale. With each breath, have them think of a color and think of as many things as possible in that color. For example, if they choose the color red, they might think of strawberries, balloons, and kites. Choose a different color for each breath.

- **My Anxiety Plan (MAP)**: Stress MAP's are anxiety management programs based on cognitive behavioral therapy. They include understanding anxiety, calming strategies, helpful thinking techniques, exposure, how to stay on track, and special topics.

- **Journaling**: Writing down feelings is an excellent way for your child to express how they are feeling, especially if it is something they don't feel comfortable saying out loud. Encourage them to journal every day, every other day, every week or whenever they feel anxious and have them write about their day, their feelings, and what they did to help themselves feel better.

- **Intensity of Feelings**: This can help you and your child assess how they are feeling during their anxiety. Have them describe how they are feeling and to make it simpler you can use a scale of one to 10 with one being least afraid to 10 being the most. This can help you pinpoint precisely how specific triggers make your child feel and give a starting point on how to reduce their anxiety at that moment.

- **Reflect on Actions**: Sometimes looking back at past actions is a good way to see how your child fell into a situation that causes anxiety, how it triggered their anxiety and what went wrong with how they handled the situation. When looking back at those situations, you can help your child figure out what they can do better the next time that situation occurs.

- **Rehearse Things Saying to Others**: This especially helps with processing thoughts in the moment of anxiety so that when your child is in a moment that they know usually causes them anxiety they know what to say and are less likely to "blank out." Have your child think of situations they are likely to face and come up with a few sentences of what they might say in those moments.

- **Write and Tear**: Writing down their feelings is a good way to have your child let out their thoughts, but writing it down and then tearing up the paper helps your child symbolically let go of those feelings. Sure, they might come back later, but it gives your child greater control over their anxiety knowing that they can kick out these feelings in this manner.

- **Worry Box**: Another way to symbolically throw away their anxious feelings, have a box like an old tissue box or shoebox and have your child write down their feelings on a piece of paper and put it in this box. This is another way of putting away their feelings and giving your child control over their anxiety.

- **Create A Character**: This gives your child a chance to flex their imagination and create a character that embodies the type of brave child they are striving to be; one that does not back down to anxiety and is equipped with all of the tools necessary to fight. This character can be a superhero, a detective, or a version of themselves that is not afraid of anxiety.

- **Thought Stopping**: This involves stopping negative thoughts right in their tracks when they occur. Your child can use counterstatements to stop them, positive self-talk, or any other technique they have learned. The idea is to end the negative thoughts before they have a chance to take hold of your child.

- **Boss Back**: This will help your child become the boss of their anxiety instead of their anxiety being the boss of them. Suppose they are in a situation where they see a dog, and they are afraid of dogs, their mind might revert to catastrophizing that the dog will hurt them and black-and-white thinking would tell them that all dogs are bad. But your child can boss back at their anxiety and say, "No, that's not true! I'm not afraid of dogs!"

- **Problem Solving**: With problem solving, your child can take a more in-depth look at what has been causing them anxiety, the thoughts they have that contribute to and solutions as to how to stop them.

- **Accept Negative Feelings**: Sometimes negative feelings occur and while there is certainly a way to combat them, understanding that they are sometimes going to happen whether your child is prepared for them or not and acceptance can be the first step to easing their anxiety.

- **Come Up With Counterstatements**: These can be very useful during anxiety triggering situations. If your child freezes during a moment of anxiety, it will be hard to come up with a counterstatement on the spot, but if they already have a few prepared, they will be better equipped to handle their anxiety when it arises. Have them write these down and practice them so they will know what to say to themselves in the future.

- **Plan Ahead**: There could be a situation in the near future that is causing much anxiety to your child. Planning would be a great way to ease some of those worries as your child will know what to do. Say, for example, your child is participating in a play at school. Plan how they will get there, what will happen when they get there, and what will happen afterward.

Exposure Therapy And How To Do It The Right Way

What Is Exposure Therapy?

In addition to cognitive behavioral therapy, another form of treatment that can help your child relieve their anxiety is exposure therapy. This is the process of assisting patients approach and engage with anxiety-provoking stimuli that pose no more than an everyday risk. Additionally, exposure therapy does not use anxiety-reducing coping skills, such as relaxation and distraction skills, explained in the previous chapter. [1]

Anxiety evoking stimuli that exposure therapy assists with can be anywhere. They can be live stimuli such as snakes and clowns or inanimate stimuli such as balloons. They can also be situational stimuli, for example, funeral homes or bridges, cognitive which might be memories of traumatic events, and finally physiological which includes factors such as a racing heartbeat or dizziness. Engagement with these anxiety-evoking stimuli can yield a response ranging from mild apprehension or intense panic.

There is some debate regarding what exactly happens in the brain during exposure therapy. What scientists agree upon, however, is that new behavior is cultivated and strengthened each time people effectively handle a previously feared situation without relying on already used safety strategies. [1]

What exposure therapy is not is throwing a person entirely into anxiety triggering a situation with no guidance and expecting them to cope with the situation on their own. The key component of exposure therapy is gradually decreasing fear of an object or a situation by putting the victim in contact with the trigger. This way, they will be able to experience anxiety in a controlled environment and learn to prevent an avoidant response. [14]

For example, some children have an irrational fear of clowns. Exposure therapy, in this case, might involve the child looking at pictures and drawings of clowns before being put in the presence of a clown directly. The next step might include playing with the props that a clown would use, such as the nose or a wig that a clown would wear. Finally, they would be put into contact with a real live clown for interaction.

Another key aspect of the treatment of anxiety disorders or phobic reactions in children is to ensure that the child is encouraged not to avoid the thing that causes them anxiety. This is why it is essential not to use coping skills during exposure therapy. Strategies such as relaxation skills can interfere with the process of habituation to anxious feelings that need to take place for exposure therapy to work. A child encouraging themselves to breathe deeply during exposure to a thing that triggers their anxiety is distancing themselves from the situation. It sends the self the message that the thing they are trying to become accustomed to is harmful and dangerous just as suspected, and this serves to counteract the exposure therapy. [14]

Also, if one of your children's strategies is to use a comfort item to deal with their anxiety, it would be a good idea to leave the item at home during the exposure therapy because it can stop the exposure therapy from working for similar reasons. Safety behaviors such as this give your child the illusion of being safe. This maintains the anxiety in the long run because the child will attribute the success of the exposure therapy to the object they brought with them for safety rather than themselves.

The Process Of Exposure Therapy

No two exposure therapies will be the same because different people have different triggers, different fear, and different levels to which these things affect them. Therefore, exposure therapy must be modified depending on the person and the particular fear trigger that affects them. However, there does not have to be a different form of exposure therapy created for each fear that the child has. The basic principles of exposure therapy can be applied to all anxiety problems. This is called a transdiagnostic approach. [1]

Essentially, the focus of exposure therapy's treatment of anxiety disorders is on the psychosocial processes that maintain the problem more so than those processes that lead to the development of the problem. There are a few reasons for this. First is that the factors that go into maintaining anxiety disorders are much better understood than those that lead to the development of the anxiety disorder.

Additionally, scientists also understand less about why some people are more vulnerable to anxiety disorders than other people. So, there is no way to change the genetic predisposition that one has to have an anxiety disorder if such an aspect is present, and there is no way to address the etiological, or developmental, factors that have to do with anxiety. [1]

However, several elements are necessary for exposure therapy to be successful and durable. One of them is that patients must be presented with information that is incompatible with their maladaptive beliefs about the dangerousness or intolerability of their anxiety trigger. As the anxiety disorder has progressed up to this point, your child may have developed maladaptive coping strategies such as rumination and catastrophizing that are not conducive to ultimately lessening their anxiety in the long run. Assuring them of the therapy and its positive abilities to reduce their anxiety is essential. [1]

Secondly, behaviors that interfere with the acquisition and consolidation of this new information must be eliminated. This goes back to not using coping strategies during exposures to objects and situations that induce anxiety, but also those maladaptive strategies, negative self-talk and thinking errors that serve to exacerbate the anxiety that your child experiences.

The final aspect that is key to successful exposure therapy is that this new information must be strengthened in memory and generalized as broadly as possible so that it is recalled in diverse contexts over time. This aspect can be developed with the practice of exposure. Like many of the strategies and therapies listed in previous chapters, it cannot be completed within one moment or one session. Practice is necessary to make the actions practiced in exposure therapy long-lasting and effective in the future. [1]

Additionally, there are a few steps that form the basis of exposure therapy treatment: [1]

- The first step to exposure therapy begins with assessment and treatment planning. In this step, the therapist, as well as the child and the parents, seek to understand the context in which the child's anxiety is triggered, the anticipated fears the child may have going into exposure therapy, of the consequences of encountering their fears, and finally the strategies that they currently use to seek safety.

- The next step of exposure therapy comes with practicing the exposure. The approach to this entirely depends on the nature of the child's fears and the goals laid out during the assessment phase for the child's exposure therapy. These also are not required to be encountered in any particular order. There are a couple of different types of exposure that can be used during this phase of the treatment. One of them is visualization, which involves exposure through the imagination, such as memories of a traumatic experience like a car accident. The other type of exposure is introspective exposure. This is when the patient elicits internal stimuli, such as engaging in physical activity to combat their fears.

- Finally, the exposure therapy concludes when the patient's expectations of danger have been reduced to the fullest possible extent. The learning is typically focused on whether the expected outcome occurred and how to follow up if it did. It is entirely possible that the fear was not eliminated and that more than one session will have to be completed. Because of this, exposure therapy can be repeated multiple times in different settings.

The Ethical Considerations Of Exposure Therapy

Despite the fact that exposure therapy has long been established as an evidence-based psychosocial treatment for anxiety disorders in children and adolescents, with over 40 randomized clinical studies supporting it, according to a study published in "Cognitive and Behavioral Practice," there are still ethical concerns raised about the use of exposure therapy, especially when it comes to children. [10]

Many therapists still hold negative views of exposure therapy or are hesitant to use exposure therapy because of the need to evoke distress in the client, which can appear to cause harm. Therapists may feel that they are damaging the child in this way, especially in clients who meet exclusionary criteria. One of the myths of exposure therapy is that it leads to a high rate of attrition and will exacerbate the symptoms of the anxiety disorder.

There are also some unique considerations to consider for the therapist when it comes to exposure therapy with children as children provide an added layer of ethical concern due to their vulnerability. The vulnerabilities that cause hesitation with working with children is that they may not understand completely what the treatment is or why facing their fears will benefit them in the long run, they were referred by someone else, and for the exposure therapy to work on children, it requires work on the part of the entire family. [10]

However, inaccurate beliefs contribute to the underutilization of a treatment proven effective, and following specific ethical guidelines can improve the delivery of treatment, especially where children are concerned.

One of those is ensuring that the child knows what is going on during the exposure therapy. Informed consent is integral to the success of exposure therapy, the study says. First, with children, the therapist must obtain permission to use exposure therapy on the child from their parent, but the child must also consent to take part in the treatment in the first place. [10]

It is also essential to provide clear and accurate information about what is going to happen during the treatment, and discussions of consent should be continually revisited throughout the treatment. At any time, the child can revoke consent to participate, and the treatment must then be modified, maybe to a lesser form of exposure, for the child to want to continue with the treatment.

Additionally, out of session work must be discussed with the child and parents as the work does not end once the session is over. Treatment must be continuous for it to be effective in the end. [10]

Naturally, there may be some hesitation on the part of the child when it comes to trying exposure therapy. After all, they will have to be facing some of their deepest fears and anxiety triggers directly. It is essential to try to frame the exposure therapy as somewhat of an experiment for the child. Inform them that it's just something to try to see if it works and come up with guesses as to how to further treat the anxiety.

Overall, there should be an emphasis on client control during the treatment as the child should be informed on exactly what the treatment will entail and that it will be collaborative between them, the exposure therapist and the parent. [10]

The Parents Role In Exposure Therapy

Although plenty of work must be done on the part of the child and the exposure therapist, responsibility also lies within the parents to assist with the child's treatment. The therapist will likely discuss boundaries and expectations going forward with the parent during the session. Parents can be excellent support for their children during exposure therapy. However, they can also unintentionally maintain the child's anxiety if they are allowing their child to continually avoid the things they are supposed to be growing accustomed to during the exposure therapy without the direction of the exposure therapist. [14]

So parents should be aware of behaviors that reinforce anxiety within their child, but they can be instrumental in encouraging exposures. There should be a balance between an empathic and supportive approach to dealing with your child's anxiety and maintaining the expectations laid out during treatment for your child's behaviors.

Also, parents should refrain from policing their child's activities and trying to catch the child doing avoidance rituals. They should also avoid deciding exposures for the child. Instead, the parent should act as a cheerleader for helping their child get through exposure therapy but never try to dictate it themselves as it should be at the discretion of the child.

With a little bit of planning, parents can get involved with exposure therapy before taking the issue to the therapist. A fun form of exposure therapy that you can do with your child right from the comfort of your home is called the Bravery Ladder. [14]

Another form of exposure therapy, the Bravery Ladder involves a hierarchy of actions. Think of climbing to the top of a ladder where the least feared aspect of confronting anxiety starts on the bottom step. As your child moves up the ladder, the action gets more difficult until they reach the highest step of the ladder where the most challenging aspect of confronting exposure therapy lies.

With your child, you will want to come up with a list of actions that can include eight to 10 items, or even more if needed. Each action must be specific and detailed. The bottom step is the action that the child can most easily master; however, don't make it so easy that it's a joke. The top step will be the hardest action. Describe the actions on the ladder in the most straightforward language possible so that the child can understand what is going to take place and what is supposed to be the result. You can note their progress by a sticker on each step because what child doesn't like stickers? [14]

If you meet resistance with your child while working on the Bravery Ladder with your child becoming too afraid to encounter their anxieties, never fear. Take a break until your child's anxiety reduces to about half of what it was initially and encourage your child to try to stick it out until the end. [14]

Most importantly, praise your child for trying and remind them that this is an essential first step in becoming accustomed to what makes them anxious. You might try easing the pressure by modifying that step on the exposure therapy to turn it into a less stressful situation. Also, give some thought into what might be causing your child's resistance to that level of exposure. Ask yourself what do they gain by staying afraid and whether there is something within the family structure that is maintaining their fear. This can be the key to freeing your child from their anxieties. [14]

Exposure therapy is an excellent tool for reducing anxiety within children. Children like exposure therapy because often they take to the idea of working their way up to eliminate their fears. Additionally, they like that exposure therapy is active and not just sitting in a room and talking about their worries with a therapist or parent.

What You Can Control Vs. What You Can't Control

Embarking On The Journey

The journey of overcoming your child's anxiety can seem overwhelming for both the parent and the child.

The child, of course, is dealing with several symptoms, physical symptoms such as increased heart rate, bodily tension, and possible anxiety attacks, as well as mental symptoms of fear and worry, in the moment of their anxiety triggers. The anxiety disorder has had an impact on the child's life leading to possible fears of going to school, interacting with peers or preventing them from participating in extracurricular activities, things that are vital to the child's development.

As a parent, your worries might lie in how you can help your child overcome their anxiety disorder. You want your child to live the best life they can without being inhibited by their disorder, but you can at times feel helpless about what to do. [14]

As you and your child embark on the journey of reducing their anxiety, it might be hard to avoid falling into the trap of worrying about things that you cannot control. However, as you go forward, it will be beneficial to both of you to put into perspective things that you can control the anxiety disorder. Focusing on things that you can control will ensure that you and your child remain motivated when tackling their anxiety disorder.

There are a lot of things that you and your child cannot control when it comes to their anxiety disorder. You cannot control what triggers their anxiety, these things are involuntary to the child, and if the child were able to choose what triggers their anxiety, they would undoubtedly want nothing. You cannot control the situations that the child encounters that trigger their anxiety as well. If your child has social anxiety and is asked to read a paper aloud in front of the class, the situation cannot be changed and falls outside of your child's control.

Your child cannot control the dreams they have about certain things or situations that make them anxious and cannot control the negative automatic thoughts that creep into their heads during the day. They also cannot control what type of treatment works for them and what doesn't. Some children might respond well to exposure therapy; for others, it does not work. Some children find smart talk to be very useful, and others would instead try something else.

Your child certainly cannot control what objects or other things trigger their anxiety and the situations that place them in a position that causes them anxiety, otherwise, the disorder would not be a problem and would not require intervention.

What Your Child Can Control

While your child's anxiety response in situations that trigger their fears, along with thinking errors and negative self-talk, is inevitable as they learn through different treatments ways to lower their anxiety, the one thing they do have control over is how they respond to their anxiety.

They can not let their anxiety disorders control them and deteriorate the quality of their life as it has been doing up to this point. As they move forward with their treatment, looking at their fears in the eyes and dealing with them, head-on can very much seem intimidating. But as your child learns various coping strategies and mental mechanisms to look at that anxiety in the face and say "you don't control me," the process will become more comfortable and your child will become more confident.

It takes time and practice to be able to move past anxiety disorders entirely, and as your child moves forward with treating their anxiety disorder, it may seem as though progress is being made too slowly.

Patience is another thing that your child has control over. Maybe they have heard time and time again that with this exposure therapy, with this smart talk, with this calming coping skill, their anxiety disorder will slowly start to disappear. Like anyone else, they may become impatient for the anxiety disorder to be over so they can live their life like a normal kid. This can ultimately become discouraging for the child.

Although children are still developing and learning skills of self-control and patience, several important factors play a role in the ability of children to wait for outcomes in a situation. Delay behavior as the child waits for future satisfaction is determined by the child's trust in the person or entity that will be presenting the outcome, relevant expectations already laid out in front of the child of the consequences to the situation, subjective values of alternatives in the situation and, finally, the rewards that come along with the outcome. [11]

Young children, particularly those up to about third grade as discussed in the study, certainly can wait for the outcome of a situation to culminate. However, certain conditions facilitate the child's ability to wait. For one thing, children can wait most effectively for gratification if, during the delay period, they can shift their attention from the gratification to occupying themselves with distractions.

In the case of an anxiety disorder, although it is something that happens to a child usually quite unexpectedly, the child can distract themselves from the disorder as well as during times when they are not in treatment or practicing a specific coping strategy such as self-talk or refreshing their use of a calming strategy. Distracting from the matter at hand can make the time between making progress go by a little bit faster. Using distraction techniques during this time would be a good strategy.

Also, self-induced conditions make for a child willingly waiting longer for an outcome. In this case, the child makes an internal note of what they are waiting for and remind themselves of it periodically but attend to less frustrating involvements or actions, giving them the ability to wait longer. With relieving anxiety disorders, the child knows that the outcome is to be free of their anxiety disorder for good, a fact that they think about now and then, but for them to be able to be patient as they work towards an outcome, they focus on something else. [11]

Finally, waiting is easier when the rewards are not in view. The study gives the example that preschool children can wait longer if they are not able to see their rewards, such as games or treats. They can wait longer when they are distracted from the rewards and thinking about the rewards when they are not in view can have a debilitating effect on the child's ability to wait. In the case of anxiety, the child may not want to think too often about the end goal of being free of the anxiety disorder, lest they become impatient for the treatment to end and stalling the progress of the treatment by possibly becoming resistant as a result. [11]

What Parents Can Control

As a parent, you have aspects of your child's anxiety that you can control as well. You can manage your involvement in the situation and how you proceed with encouraging your child to overcome the disorder. There are several different types of parenting, most of which can end up being detrimental to your child relieving their anxiety. [14]

Permissive parents allow too much to slide by and do not set enough boundaries. Authoritative parents, in contrast, set too many boundaries against their child. You want to avoid over-parenting and under-parenting as they can adversely affect the child's coping skills and serve to increase their anxiety. [14]

Additionally, there is a decent correlation between the type of parenting used and the development of anxiety disorders in children. It has to do with the psychological granting of autonomy to your child, or rejection of your child, versus the psychological control that you establish over your child.

Projecting rejectionist actions over your child involves exhibiting low levels of parental warmth approval and responsiveness. These can come in the form of coldness, disapproval, and unresponsiveness. It can be disguised as giving your child more autonomy over themselves but results in your child missing out on the much-needed guidance of a parent and in the end, putting the child at increased risk for anxiety.

Conversely, exhibiting too much control over your child involves excessive regulation of routines, encouragement of dependence on the parents, and instruction on how the child should think or feel. This results in decreased self-efficacy and increased anxiety. [14]

The path you want to follow as a parent should, again, be one of balance. Ultimately, encouragement of autonomy and independence increases the child's perception of mastery over their environment, which leads to a reduction in anxiety.

Instead of reacting to your child's anxiety disorder with an increased need for control over them or a perceived lack of interest, you want to find a good balance with your involvement in your child's anxiety disorder by striving to be the attentive parent. Here you are sensitive to your child's inclinations and needs and can adjust your responses from protective to encouraging as needed. Find your control of the difficult path to relieving your child's anxiety disorder by reacting with a balance of emotions that will help you to encourage your child better to keep trying.

How To Move On

You've studied the causes of anxiety and gained some insight into what might be bothering your child. You have introduced to them several coping skills and techniques to ease their anxieties. You may be considering taking your child to a therapist, or you already have and have seen results through some treatments such as cognitive behavioral therapy or exposure therapy. Your child may have been able to eliminate their anxiety completely or is still in the process of doing so.

Now the critical question is, what happens next? How do you move forward from this point on?

Following the treatment of anxiety, it is important to be realistic about your expectations for your child. If your child was timid before treating anxiety, you should not expect them to be the life of the party now that their anxiety has been dealt with. If they were introverted, don't expect them to become very extroverted, and vice versa. If that kind of dramatic change happens, that's great. But your child is still the same child following successful treatment of their anxiety; the only difference is that anxiety no longer rules their life. Expecting a complete personality shift is unrealistic. [14]

What may occur is that your child might have a relapse where they revert to old patterns of behavior before their treatment for anxiety. Symptom fluctuations can happen during times of situational stress, which can bring about old fears where your child thinks that danger is likely.

Progress is not something that happens overnight. It can be a long journey that can start and stop unpredictably. Some children take huge steps during anxiety treatment, while some only take small steps. Some have a combination of both. Remember, it likely took a long time for your child's anxiety to develop, so it is unrealistic to expect the anxiety to dissolve overnight.

As a parent, don't be too concerned about the setbacks. Understand that they might happen, but you have the tools necessary to help bring your child back up to speed. This is also important because children can pick up on the worries of their parents, which can contribute to the likelihood of them having a relapse. Or it can lead to avoidant behavior in other circumstances that were not a problem in the past.

Instead of worrying about your child experiencing setbacks in their journey to overcome anxiety, remind them of the progress that they have made up to this point which will encourage them to keep progressing and relieve some of your worries as a parent. [71]

Maybe you have been handling your child's anxiety on your own, and you don't feel like progress is being made, or it is not being made at the pace that you hoped to achieve. It may be a good idea to involve an outside party in a few different situations, Pincus says. If your child experiences extreme responses to stressful situations, their life is not improving with only parental intervention. The general functioning of the family is being undermined by your child's difficulties, or their teacher suggests seeing a therapist then it might be time. [14]

However, involving a therapist can serve as an extra motivator for your child and provide a springboard for even more change. If you do decide to take your child to a therapist, ensure that whoever you choose is trained in cognitive behavioral therapy skills and is also specialized in working with children.

One thing that often gets overlooked but is still of great importance is tracking your child's progress throughout therapy and beyond. Traditionally, we tend to base progress on the changing of symptoms from pre- to post-treatment. However, this way of thinking neglects the essential intermediate steps for therapeutic change. [11]

It is vital to understand not how treatment has worked from beginning to end but measuring progress at the steps in between will help to know when exactly treatment is occurring, not just when it is over. It will allow you to see when the shift in your child's behaviors begins to occur and provides a better understanding of how such therapy works.

To better track your child's progress, measure the change in your child from each session you work with them. Sometimes there may be very little change during one session, but write it down anyway, and when your child makes immense leaps in their progress for reducing their anxiety, it will be easier to see what is happening. Additionally, it will help identify what elements of treatment are contributing to the change so that you can continue those actions while you can put less emphasis on the ones that are not helping as much. [11]

Most importantly, you want to keep your child's progress going. You both have come this far and did all of this work, so ensuring that progress continues will help to prevent future setbacks. Reinforcing the warm connection, you have between your child can be an excellent place to start, as you are your child's biggest supporter. Continue to be a model of positive reinforcement for your child and continue to do small practices each day to maintain what your child has learned. After all, treatment is an ongoing practice, and progress can only be made if the work continues beyond therapy sessions and work sessions at home. [11]

Encourage your child to keep challenging themselves. It may even be a good idea to involve loved ones, such as grandparents and other family members. Children respond to consistency and predictability, and all of these things will be beneficial to them in the long run.

Finally, remember to celebrate your child's successes. Encouragement is going to be the most crucial aspect of keeping your child going through their anxiety treatment. To them, this may be very difficult, they may be afraid, but with your encouragement and praise of every milestone they take, it will help them see that what they are doing is worthwhile and that everything will be okay in the long run. [14]

Conclusion

Anxiety disorders come in many different forms from general anxiety disorders, social anxiety, panic disorder, and more, and can be debilitating for anyone who experiences them. They affect a person's quality of life, preventing them from going into an everyday situation with a clear mind.

Anxiety disorders can particularly impact children as they are still in an important developmental stage where imagination, discovery and new experiences are essential for ensuring that they grow into a well-rounded individual who can be successful in adulthood. Anxiety can prevent them from embarking on such new experiences and inhibit the quality of their childhood.

As a parent, you want what is best for your child. You want to give them the quality of life that they need and deserve to have a normal childhood. Their anxiety disorder can be a source of discouragement and stress for a parent as well, but doing the research and learning everything you can about what your child is experiencing and what you can do to help is a good step to take.

External stimuli such as objects and life situations as well as internal actions such as cognitive delusions, negative automatic thoughts, and negative self-talk are all contributors to anxiety, but the possibilities of ways your child can cope with your anxiety are seemingly endless. From smart talk, cognitive behavioral therapy, exposure therapy and dozens of coping skills such as calming skills and distraction skills, there is something for everyone to try and more than likely help to put a stop to their anxiety.

Despite the endless techniques and skills that your child can acquire to relieve their anxiety, the most important thing they can have is the support of a parent. Anxiety disorders and the road to recovery can be scary and overwhelming for a child, but having the support of a parent to help them along the way learning and practicing the various anxiety-reducing techniques can be the encouragement they need not to give up and keep powering through to end their anxiety once and for all.

References

1. Abramowitz, Jonathan S. Deacon, Brett J. Whiteside, Stephen P. H. (2019). *Exposure Therapy for Anxiety: Principles and Practice, Second Edition.*

2. Ankowski, Amber. (2019). "Inspiring Your Child's Imagination." *PBS.*

3. "Cognitive Skills for Anxiety." *University of Michigan.*

4. Davidson, Gerald C. Feldman, Peter M. Osborn, Carl E. (1984). "Articulated Thoughts, Irrational Beliefs, and Fear of Negative Evaluation." *Cognitive Therapy and Research.*

5. "Distraction Techniques." (2016). *NeuRA.*

6. Egan, Kieran. Judson, Gillian. (2015). "Imagination and the Engaged Learner: Cognitive Tools for the Classroom."

7. Flynn Walker, Bridgett. (2017). *Anxiety Relief for Kids: On-The-Spot Strategies to Help Your Child Overcome Worry, Panic & Avoidance.*

8. Gavinski, Igor. Markman, Keith D. McMullen, Matthew N. Sherman, Steven J. (1995). "The Impact of Perceived Control on the Imagination of Better and Worse Possible Worlds." *The Society for Personality and Social Psychology, Inc.*

9. Goddard, Colleen. (2014). "More Than Just Teddy Bears." *Psychology Today.*

10. Gola, Jennifer A. Beidas, Rinad S. Antinoro-Burke, Diana. Kratz, Hilary E. Fingerhut, Randy. (2016). "Ethical Considerations in Exposure

Therapy With Children." *Cognitive Behavioral Practice.*

11. Hayes, Sarah A. Miller, Nathan A. Hope, Debra A. Heimberg, Richard G. Juster, Harlan R. (2008). "Assessing Client Progress Session by Session in the Treatment of Social Anxiety Disorder: The Social Anxiety Session Change Index." *Cognitive Behavioral Practice.*

12. Healthwise Staff. (2018). "Anxiety: Stop Negative Thoughts." Michigan Medicine University of Michigan.

13. Hurley, Katie. "5 Ways To Calm An Anxious Child." *Psychom.*

14. Pincus, Donna B. (2012). *Growing Up Brave: Expert Strategies for Helping Your Child Overcome Fear, Stress and Anxiety.*

15. Legerstee, Jereon S. Jellesman, Francine C. Utens, Elizabeth M. W. J. (2009). "Cognitive Coping and Childhood Anxiety Disorders." *European Childhood Adolescent Psychiatry.*

16. Martinelli, Katherine. "How to Help Kids Who Are Too Hard on Themselves." *The Child Mind Institute.*

17. Modell, Arnold H. (2003). *Imagination and the Meaningful Brain.*

18. Ollendick, Thomas H. Seligman, Laura D. (2012). "Cognitive Behavioral Therapy for Anxiety Disorders in Youth." *U.S. National Library of Medicine National Institutes of Health.*

19. "Relaxation." *University of Michigan.*

20.   Strawson, P.F. "Imagination and Perception."

21. Taylor, Shelley. (1998). "Coping Strategies." *The John D. and Katherine T. MacArthur Foundation.*

22.   "Understanding the Facts of Anxiety Disorders and Depression is the First Step." *Anxiety and Depression Association of America.*

23.   The Understood Team. "Slow Processing Speed and Anxiety: What You Need to Know."

24.   Waller, Diane. (2006). "Art Therapy for Children: How It Leads to Change." *Clinical Psychology and Psychiatry.*

25.   Wood, Jeffrey J. (2006). "Family Involvement in Cognitive-Behavioral Therapy for Children's Anxiety Disorders." *Psychiatric Times.*

26. Zinbarg, Richard E. "What Is an Anxiety Disorder?" *American Psychological Association.*

Disclaimer

The information contained in this book and its components, is meant to serve as a comprehensive collection of strategies that the author of this book has done research about. Summaries, strategies, tips and tricks are only recommendations by the author, and reading this book will not guarantee that one's results will exactly mirror the author's results.

The author of this book has made all reasonable efforts to provide current and accurate information for the readers of this book. The author and its associates will not be held liable for any unintentional errors or omissions that may be found.

The material in the book may include information by third parties. Third party materials comprise of opinions expressed by their owners. As such, the author of this book does not assume responsibility or liability for any third party material or opinions.

The publication of third party material does not constitute the author's guarantee of any information, products, services, or opinions contained within third party material. Use of third party material does not guarantee that your results will mirror our results. Publication of such third party material is simply a recommendation and expression of the author's own opinion of that material.

Whether because of the progression of the Internet, or the unforeseen changes in company policy and editorial submission guidelines, what is stated as fact at the time of this writing may become outdated or inapplicable later.

written expressed and signed permission from the author.

CPSIA information can be obtained
at www.ICGtesting.com
Printed in the USA
LVHW090335101219
640002LV00002B/237/P

9 781646 960064